Dining During the Depression

Strong family ties, hard work and good old-fashioned cooking sustained folks through the 1930s. These are the recipes—and precious memories—of those who lived through the Great Depression.

REMINISCE BOOKS

3

Editor: Karen Thibodeau
Assistant Editors: Julie Buchsbaum,
Mike Beno
Art Director: Maribeth Greinke
Art Associates: Stephanie Marchese,
Jim Sibilski, Bonnie Ziolecki
Editorial Assistants: Joe Kertzman,
Blanche Comiskey
Production Assistants: Judy Pope,
Ellen Lloyd, Julie Wagner
Publisher: Roy J. Reiman

©1996, Reiman Publications, L.P.
5400 S. 60th St., Greendale WI 53129

Reminisce Books
International Standard Book Number:
0-89821-156-5
Library of Congress Catalog Card
Number: 95-72660

For additional copies of this book or information on other books, write: Reminisce Books,
P.O. Box 990, Greendale WI 53129. **Credit card orders call toll-free 1-800/558-1013.**

CONTENTS

INTRODUCTION

NO MATTER WHERE folks lived during the Depression—on the farm or in the city—hard work and family togetherness got them through those tough times.

Fathers worked the land to keep food on the table or took whatever jobs they could find, regardless of how low the pay.

Mothers used ingenuity to make tasty and nutritious meals out of the most basic ingredients, devising creative substitutes when foods were scarce.

Children were also big contributors and no effort was too small. They tended gardens, helped "put up" produce to last through the cold winters, hunted game and pitched in with cooking chores.

Everyone was called on to do his or her part and family members depended on each other. Grandparents, aunts, uncles and cousins were close at hand too, and Sundays were often spent around the table sharing simple fare that the whole family helped in some way to prepare.

Dishes from those days weren't fancy. Those plain-but-pleasing foods lacked today's convenience, but they were still mighty good. The ingredients were cheap, simple and, whenever possible, home-grown. Nothing was wasted and food was stretched as far as it could go—then stretched a little bit further.

Included in the eight chapters of this book are some of the common dishes of those days, contributed by those who knew them best—the folks who were sustained by them in the 1930s.

To convey the flavor of daily life during those years, the recipes in this book appear as they did in the contributors' letters. Some copied their recipes from cards they inherited from mothers and grandmothers. Others put together the directions from memory. After all, many cooks of the day didn't bother putting recipes down on paper. They cooked by feel—adding a pinch of this and a handful of that.

Just reading through the recipes will give you a taste of the times. If you should choose to try some of the dishes, keep these things in mind:

(1) The recipes included in this book have not been tested by Reiman Publications' test kitchens. In order to present these Depression-era recipes just as they came from our readers recipe files, we did not "modernize" them by adjusting ingredients or cooking times.

(2) Ingredient amounts, cooking times and temperatures may be approximate or, in some cases, not included. Many of the recipes were intended to be made in wood stoves and cooks of the day learned by experience how long and at what temperature to prepare foods.

(3) Most of the dairy products, vegetables, poultry, eggs and meats used were those that families grew and raised themselves. In some cases, contributors have substituted more convenient modern versions of these items and other ingredients.

In addition to recipes, you'll find lots of special memories about this no-frills fare that helped families brave the lean years.

Children and grandchildren of these American pioneers may wonder how their ancestors got by on foods like Poor Man's Steak, Black-Eyed Pea Sausage, Dandelion Greens and Vinegar Pie. But to them it was easy—their meals were flavored with love.

Dig right in and enjoy your look back!

Chapter 1

Vegetables and Salads

Gardens got families through with plentiful produce to eat fresh or "put up" for the winter.

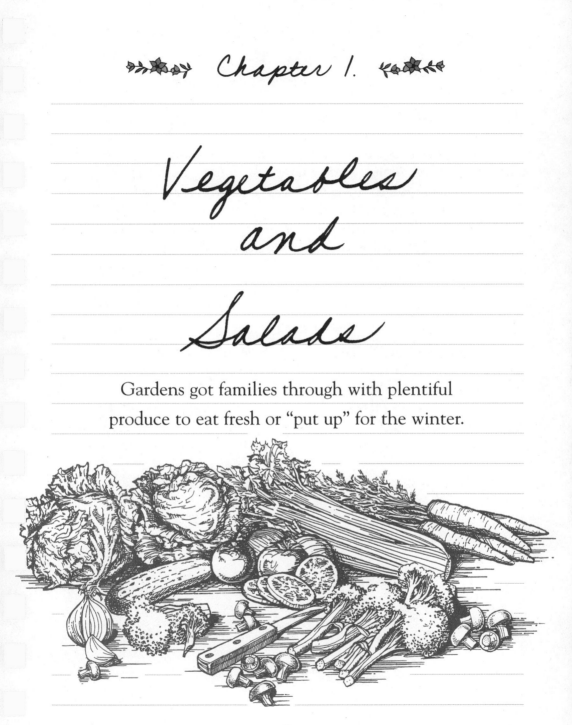

Black-Eyed Pea Sausage

Shared by Faye McLain, Dallas, Georgia

I GREW UP in the Arkansas Delta, in the bottomland between the Mississippi and St. Francis Rivers.

The Depression years were hard, but what wonderful memories! We raised hogs on our farm, but they were sold to bring us enough money for clothes and shoes. Mother found other ways to make sure we didn't go hungry.

She grew a large garden and we'd pick the black-eyed peas, put them in sacks and beat them on a tree or the ground to shell them. We'd have black-eyed peas for supper that night and Mother would save the leftovers, putting them in a syrup bucket and lowering them into the well so they'd stay cold.

The next day, she'd make our favorite Black-Eyed Pea Sausage. If there was any left over, my sister and I would take it to school in our lunches that Mother packed in another old syrup bucket.

2 cups black-eyed peas, cooked, cold
1 egg
1/2 cup self-rising flour
1-1/2 teaspoons sage
1 teaspoon red pepper, crushed
1/2 teaspoon salt
1/2 teaspoon black pepper
Shortening

Mix all ingredients well. Form into small patties. Fry in small amount of shortening in iron skillet or nonstick pan.

Poke Salad

Shared by Helen Tullock, Delano, Tennessee

A picking of pokeweed
Water
    3 to 4 slices bacon, fried
    3 to 4 eggs
Salt

Boil the pokeweed in at least two changes of water. When it is tender, add to bacon drippings in the skillet in which the bacon was cooked. Add the eggs, one at a time, and scramble them with the pokeweed until well cooked. Add salt to taste. Bacon bits may also be added.

Dandelions in Ham Gravy

Shared by Doris Stackhouse, Bourbon, Indiana

Bacon fryings *or* shortening
    3 rounded tablespoons flour
    1 slice ham, diced
    4 tablespoons white sugar
    2 tablespoons white vinegar
Water, enough for thick gravy
    1 quart dandelions,
       cleaned and cut into
       2-inch lengths
Potato, boiled, diced, optional
Egg, hard-boiled, diced, optional

Melt shortening or bacon fryings in a skillet. Add flour and ham. Brown to desired color, stirring occasionally so it won't scorch. Remove skillet from burner and add sugar and vinegar. Mix in 1/2 cup of water. Return skillet to burner and add more water to make a thick gravy. Remove skillet from burner, toss dandelions in gravy and serve at once so dandelions will not wilt. Add potato or hard-boiled egg, if desired. **Yield:** 2 servings.

Scalloped Turnips

Shared by Debbie Jones, California, Maryland

4 cups turnips, cooked
4 tablespoons sugar
Salt and pepper to taste
4 eggs, slightly beaten

2-1/2 cups bread crumbs
1 stick margarine

Mix ingredients together. Bake at 375° for 1 hour.

'Punkin Blooms'

Shared by Mildred Snyder, Gray, Tennessee

False pumpkin blossoms
Cornmeal
Water
Salt

Carefully pick the false pumpkin blossoms. Do not choose those with a pumpkin shape on the end.

Wash pumpkin blossoms, then let stand in salted water for about 30 minutes. Drain pumpkin blossoms and roll them in cornmeal. Fry in fat, turning so that both sides brown. Poke stalks or wild mushrooms can be substituted for pumpkin blossoms, if desired.

Parsnip Fritters

Shared by Alberta Price, Hagerstown, Maryland

4 parsnips, boiled
1/4 teaspoon salt
1 teaspoon flour
1 egg, beaten

Scrape the skins off of the raw parsnips. Boil until done in as little water as possible. Mash and season with salt. Add the flour and egg. Form into small cubes and fry in a little oil until well browned on both sides.

Shared by Mary Lund, South Stoddard, New Hampshire

Bulrush *or* cattails
Water
Butter
Salt and pepper to taste

Gather in late spring before flower-spike has turned brown and sausage-like. Flower is encased in its long green leaf. To prepare it for cooking, peel as you would corn. Put flowers into boiling salted water for about 10 minutes. Dip in melted butter, then salt and pepper to taste. Nibble the outside of flowers (the inside is a hard core).

Bean Cakes Were Good Meat Substitute Then—and Now

LEFTOVER beans never went to waste in our house. Mom made them into bean cakes for our school lunches.

She'd mash the beans, mix them with flour and fry them until they were nice and brown. She used lard sparingly since during much of the year she had to buy it.

Though the Depression years are long gone, I still make bean cakes occasionally. My sons, and now my grandchildren, really enjoy them.

I saw a recipe in the newspaper recently that was a lot like Mom's bean cakes. They called them "bean burgers" and said they were a good meat substitute—my mother knew that 60 years ago!

—Georgia Mae Nicholson, French Lick, Indiana

Turnip Roots

Shared by Sara Lindler, Irmo, South Carolina

6 to 8 large turnips
1 to 2 cups water
1/2 pound fresh pork
Salt and pepper to taste
1 tablespoon sugar
1/4 teaspoon ginger, optional

Wash turnip roots and peel skin off. Be sure to cut deeply enough to remove skin. Cut or dice turnips. Put in pot with water. Add pork and seasonings. Cook about 30 minutes or until pork is done.

Carrot Salad

Shared by Shirley Heiden, Black Creek, Wisconsin

2 cups carrots, grated
1 small onion, chopped
1/2 green pepper, chopped
1/4 teaspoon salt
1/4 head lettuce, finely chopped

Boiled Salad Dressing
4 eggs
1 cup sugar
1/2 teaspoon salt
Pepper
1 tablespoon cornstarch

1 cup vinegar
Whipped cream

Mix first five ingredients together. Set aside. For dressing, beat eggs, then add sugar, salt and pepper. Dissolve cornstarch in some of the vinegar. Boil in double boiler until thick. When cool, add equal amount of whipped cream. Add 2 tablespoons dressing to vegetables, toss and serve.

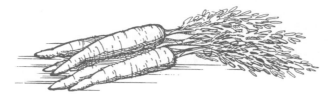

Dilled Poke Stems or Okra

Shared by Kathy Phillips, Glendale, Arizona

WE LIVED next to a railroad track in a small town in Oklahoma. My mother knew that in the rich soil there grew a number of nutritious, tasty plants that many consider weeds today.

Pokeweed was one of the greens we often ate. The stems could be sliced, battered and fried for a delicious vegetable similar to fried okra.

Pokeweed leaves were long and wide and you didn't have to pick very much to have a nice "mess" of it. The stems could also be pickled for a treat similar to pickled okra.

We usually found pokeweed in the early spring after a lot of rain or along the river banks where there was plenty of moisture.

We also ate a lot of dandelion greens and lamb's-quarters in those days. The dandelions were only good if you picked the lightest colored leaves. The darker the leaf, the more bitter the flavor. Lamb's-quarters were plentiful most of the year and were my favorite.

Our cabinets weren't always full, but we never went hungry!

Pokeweed
- 1 clove garlic
- 2 heads dill
- 1 teaspoon alum

Brine
- 1 cup vinegar
- 2 cups water
- 1 teaspoon salt

Cut stems 3 to 4 inches long. To each sterilized quart jar add garlic, dill and alum. For each quart of pickles prepare brine of vinegar, water and salt. Bring brine to a boil and pour over pokeweed or okra stems. Seal with new canning lids.

Garden Helped Produce Lots of Sandwiches

MY MOTHER *could make a sandwich out of anything. During the Depression, a popular Sunday supper at our house was a sandwich made of the cold mashed potatoes from our noon meal. It was topped with slices of Bermuda onions from our garden and seasoned with salt and pepper. Of course the bread was homemade and so was the butter.*

But the family favorite was peanut butter and tomato sandwiches. In those days, peanut butter was sold in bulk. You dipped what you wanted out of larger cans and the amount was weighed in a paper "boat". You could get a "boatful" of peanut butter—about a pound— for a nickel.

The tomatoes for our sandwiches were always grown in our garden and Mother sliced them about 1/4-inch thick. She'd top them with salt and pepper, then spread homemade butter on one slice of homemade bread. She'd cover the other slice with peanut butter.

Anyone who visited our house for lunch was served this sandwich. It was cheap, filling and tasty.

To this day, peanut butter and tomato sandwiches are still one of my favorites. I, too, serve them to guests. Those game enough to try them are always surprised at how delicious they taste!

—Dorothy Farrell, Topeka, Kansas

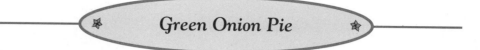

Green Onion Pie

Shared by Precious Owens, Elizabethtown, Kentucky

3 cups green onions
3 tablespoons butter
2 eggs
1/2 cup cream
1 teaspoon salt
1/8 teaspoon pepper
1 9-inch pie pastry

Pick young, fresh green onions and wash them thoroughly. Make a 9-inch pie pastry and line a pie plate with it. Saute green onions in butter until tender. Arrange onions on pastry. Beat eggs slightly. Add cream, salt and pepper. Mix well. Pour mixture over onions. Bake at 425° for 18 to 20 minutes or until well browned and knife inserted in center comes out clean.

Depression Salad

Shared by Bernice Davis, Moore, Oklahoma

1 15-1/2-ounce can yellow
   hominy, drained
1 15-1/2-ounce can black-
   eyed peas, drained
1 green pepper, chopped
1 tomato, chopped
1 small onion, chopped
2 ribs celery, diced
1/4 cup cooking oil, optional
1/4 cup vinegar
Salt and pepper to taste

Mix ingredients well and serve.

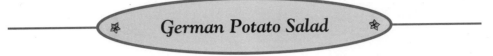

German Potato Salad

Shared by Nancy Reed, Birmingham, Alabama

8 to 10 red potatoes
1 onion, chopped
1 cucumber, sliced
6 tablespoons salad oil
6 tablespoons vinegar
6 tablespoons hot water
Salt and pepper
Hard-boiled eggs, sliced
Tomato wedges

Boil potatoes, then place them in a bowl of cold water to cool. Peel skins off potatoes and slice. Add onion and cucumber. Set aside. Mix salad oil, vinegar and hot water together and pour mixture over potatoes. Salt and pepper to taste. Garnish with slices of hard-boiled eggs and tomato wedges.

Grandpa's Sweet-Sour Slaw

Shared by Virginia Elliott, Naples, Florida

3 cups cabbage, finely grated
1 small onion, finely grated
1 green pepper, grated
1/4 cup water
1/3 cup cider vinegar
2 rounded tablespoons sugar
1 teaspoon celery seed
1 teaspoon caraway seed
1 teaspoon salt
1 rounded tablespoon coarse black pepper

Using slaw slicer or food processor, grate cabbage very finely until you have 3 cups. Grate onion and green pepper. In a large bowl, combine grated cabbage, onion and green pepper. In a small bowl, mix water, vinegar, sugar, celery seed, caraway seed, salt and black pepper. Mash and stir this mixture with the back of a wooden spoon for about 2 minutes and pour over the slaw mixture. The longer it stands, the better. Toss mixture often.

Dad's Bedtime Snack Left Lingering Impression

THOUGH I WAS only a young child during the '30s, I can still remember the smell of the onion sandwiches my dad loved to eat.

Right before the nightly news on the radio, Dad would head to the kitchen for his bedtime snack. He'd spread two pieces of bread with butter, layer thin slices of Vidalia or Bermuda onions on top, then add salt and pepper and dig in. Dad grew marvelous tomatoes in his garden, so he'd occasionally slice one up to pile on his favorite snack.

Dad thought those sandwiches were the best. Our family thought they were the worst. We could still smell the onions when we sat down to breakfast! —Julie Shields, Hartland, Wisconsin

Corn Bread-Tomato Goop

Shared by Bobbie Napper, Tomball, Texas

1-1/2 tablespoons bacon grease or oil
1/4 cup green pepper, chopped
1/4 cup onion, chopped
1 16-ounce can diced peeled tomatoes
1/3 cup water
1 tablespoon sugar
1 teaspoon chili powder
1/2 teaspoon black pepper
1-1/2 cups leftover corn bread, crumbled

In a large skillet, saute onion and pepper in bacon grease until limp. Add tomatoes, water, sugar, chili powder and black pepper. Bring to a boil. Reduce heat to simmer for 10 minutes. Mix in corn bread. Serve hot (but it's also good cold).

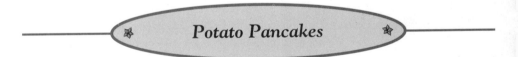

Milkweed Pods

Shared by Mary Lund, South Stoddard, New Hampshire

WHEN I WAS a little girl, my grandmother would take me out early in the morning to help pick milkweed greens. They were ready to be picked when they were about as high as a young girl's waist or an adult's knees.

You could only pick the top three leaves though—the lower leaves were too bitter to eat.

It took a long time to pick a basketful, and then they had to be cleaned. We always put them in a kettle of boiling water with a piece of salt pork and then added plenty of peeled potatoes. We topped that dish with vinegar and enjoyed it at many suppers.

Milkweed pods, washed
Water
Salt and pepper
Grated cheese
Butter

Gather pods about mid-August when they are dusty green and 1 to 1-1/2 inches long. Salt some water and bring to a boil. Toss the washed pods in and boil for about 10 minutes. Test to make sure they are tender. When you take them out, strain them and place them in a hot dish. Sprinkle with salt and pepper. Top with grated cheese, if desired. A dab of butter on each pod is a real treat.

Potato Pancakes

Shared by Marlene Boddie, Williamson, Georgia

1 **quart potatoes, finely grated**
2 **large eggs,** *separated*
Salt to taste
1 **small onion, grated**

Mix potatoes, egg yolks, salt and onion. Beat egg whites, then fold into potato mixture. In a heavy skillet, fry by dropping heaping spoonfuls into hot oil.

18

Shared by Lillian Flanum, Clear Lake, Wisconsin

1 **quart corn, grated off the cob**
1 **cup milk**
1-1/2 **teaspoons salt**
1/4 **teaspoon pepper**
1 **cup flour**
1 **teaspoon baking powder**
4 **eggs, well beaten**
Butter

In a 1-1/2- to 2-quart bowl, combine the grated corn, milk, salt and pepper. Mix well. Add baking powder to flour and stir into the corn mixture. Blend in beaten eggs and stir well. Melt butter in a frying pan. Drop mixture by large spoonfuls into the pan and fry slowly until one side is brown. Turn and brown other side, so raw corn cooks through. Serve hot with butter.

Dad's Bean Crop Made Meals for Prisoners

DURING THE Depression my grandfather supplemented his income by growing and selling navy beans to the county jail in Towanda, Pennsylvania.

In those days, prisoners were fed plain oatmeal for breakfast and usually bologna and beans during the mid-afternoon.

When the jail population was down, we ate beans prepared in many ways and my favorite was my grandmother's bean soup.
It's still my favorite after 60 years!
—Francis Benjamin,
D'Iberville, Mississippi

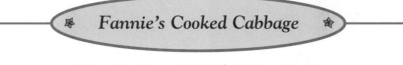

Fannie's Cooked Cabbage

Shared by Leona Pifer, Interlachen, Florida

1 2-1/2- to 3-pound head cabbage
3 to 4 cups water
1 tablespoon salt
2 slices bacon, diced
1/2 cup flour
1/4 cup vinegar

Slice cabbage and put in a pot. Add water and salt. Cover pot and boil cabbage until tender, about 1 hour. In a small frying pan, fry diced bacon until crisp. Take bacon out and add flour to bacon grease. Fry flour in bacon grease until very brown. Flour may be lumpy. Add to the pot of cabbage. Mix well, then add vinegar and cook 10 to 15 minutes more. Add more salt if desired.

Hopping John

Shared by Marion Tammany, Reno, Nevada

1 cup cowpeas *or* black-eyed peas
1/4 cup bacon, cut in pieces
1 cup rice
4 cups water
Salt to taste
Onion, optional

Boil peas and bacon together in water. When peas are tender, stir in the rice and salt and cook until all water is absorbed. If you have an onion, chop onion finely and add to the peas and bacon to cook. **Yield:** 4 to 6 servings.

Saturday Night Skillet

Shared by Irene King, Uniontown, Pennsylvania

Carrots
Onion, chopped
Dry bread cubes
Salt and pepper
Bacon grease

Vary the proportions of ingredients according to the number of people being served. Wash carrots and cook them about 10 to 12 minutes. Peel and slice. Melt bacon grease in a skillet and add carrots, chopped onion and dry bread cubes. Salt and pepper to taste. Cover skillet and steam about 1/2 hour. Keep stirring and mix well.

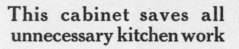

This cabinet saves all unnecessary kitchen work

EVERYTHING is at your fingers' ends—saves countless steps and avoids the disagreeable part of getting meals and clearing up afterwards.

The Hoosier Kitchen Cabinet is used three times every day by 300,000 women, thousands situated as you are, who would not now think of getting along without it.

Try one for 30 days yourself in your own kitchen.

You will take less steps, be less tired and have less waste.

Write for our handsome catalogue. It tells why it is easier to buy the Hoosier and be sure it is the most convenient, than it is to buy an unknown cabinet and take chances.

Our terms and prices are so liberal you will never miss the little money the cabinet costs—besides **saving $5 to $15 in actual value on it.**

Special Offer to women in towns where we have no dealer. Write us about it.

The Hoosier Manufacturing Company, 50 Adams St., New Castle, Ind.
223 Pacific Bldg., San Francisco, Cal.

More Hoosiers in use than all other makes combined.

Dorothy Warfield

22

Harvard Beets

Shared by Deborah DePoy, Mill Creek, Indiana

AS A *farmer's daughter, my mother learned to cook from her mother and the neighbor ladies who prepared meals for the threshers.*

Those hardworking men appreciated good home-cooked dinners that stuck to their ribs. Grandma often served them fried chicken with cream gravy and biscuits, along with our family favorite, Harvard Beets.

During her childhood days, my mom learned well how to feed a hungry crew and later, when I was growing up, no one ever left our home hungry. She was always concerned her guests didn't get enough to eat and after a big meal often asked, "Are you sure I can't fix you a hamburger or something?"

3 cups beets, cooked and diced
1/2 cup beet juice
1/2 cup water
3 tablespoons cornstarch
2 tablespoons sugar
1 teaspoon salt
Dash pepper
1/3 cup vinegar

Heat beets, beet juice and water. Combine cornstarch, sugar, salt, pepper and vinegar. Add to beets and stir constantly until smooth, blended and thickened. **Yield:** 6 servings.

Cabbage Salad

Shared by Deborah Mors, Brooks, Maine

1 medium head cabbage, shredded
1/4 cup mayonnaise
1/2 cup sugar
2 large carrots, shredded
1 large onion, sliced
1 cup vinegar
Salt and pepper, optional

Mix the cabbage, carrots and onion. Set aside. Combine mayonnaise, vinegar, sugar and salt and pepper if desired. Blend with vegetables and serve.

Baked Kale with Potatoes

Shared by Janet Flower, Portland, Oregon

9 tablespoons butter,
  softened, *divided*
3 pounds kale
1/2 pound lean bacon,
  coarsely diced
1/2 cup beef stock, fresh *or*
  canned
2 teaspoons salt, *divided*
1/4 teaspoon ground nutmeg
9 medium boiling potatoes
  (about 3 pounds), peeled
  and cut into 1/2-inch cubes
1/2 to 3/4 cup milk
Fresh ground black pepper
2 egg yolks
Water

With a pastry brush, coat the bottom and sides of an 8- x 10-inch baking dish with 1 tablespoon of butter. Set the dish aside. Wash the kale thoroughly. Cut away the ends and tough stems as well as any bruised or yellow leaves. Cover kale in lightly salted water and boil for 10 minutes. Drain thoroughly in a colander. Press it firmly with the back of a spoon to remove any excess liquid. Chop the kale coarsely. In a heavy 4- to 5-quart saucepan, cook the bacon over moderate heat until it is crisp and brown. Add the kale, turning it with a large spoon until the leaves are coated with fat. Stir in the beef stock, 1 teaspoon salt and nutmeg and bring to a boil over high heat. Reduce the heat to low and simmer uncovered for 20 minutes, stirring occasionally. Preheat oven to 400°. Cover potatoes with lightly salted water and boil until tender but not falling apart. Drain, return to pan and shake over low heat for 2 to 3 minutes until dry. Force potatoes through a food mill/ricer over a bowl. Beat 6 tablespoons at a time, using enough milk to make a puree that holds shape in a spoon. Beat in the remaining teaspoon of salt, a few grindings of black pepper, 6 tablespoons of butter and the egg yolks, one at a time. Taste for seasoning, adding more if desired. Spread cooked kale evenly over the bottom of the prepared baking dish. Smooth the potatoes over it and dot the top with the remaining 2 tablespoons of butter. Bake for 20 minutes or until the surface of the potatoes is golden brown. Serve at once directly from baking dish.

Vegetable Pudding

Shared by Lillian Marcotte, Woodstock, Vermont

1 cup carrots, grated
1 cup potatoes, grated
1 cup flour
1 cup sugar
1 rounded teaspoon baking
    soda
Cloves
Nutmeg
Cinnamon

Finely grate carrots and potatoes. Combine ingredients and steam for 3 hours. Serve cold with whipped cream or prepare Foamy Sauce using recipe below.

Foamy Sauce
  1/2 cup brown sugar
    1 egg, *separated*
  1/4 cup hot milk
Vanilla

Combine sugar and egg yolk. Pour hot milk over mixture and beat with an egg beater. Add vanilla to taste, then stir in stiffly beaten egg white.

Fried Locust Blooms Were Tasty 'Survival Food'

LIVING IN West Virginia, there were several "survival foods" we ate a lot of during the Depression.

In addition to fried pumpkin blooms and poke stalks, we also ate fried locust blooms.

When a locust tree blossoms, it produces tiny clusters of blooms. We'd pick and separate the blooms and then wash them. Next, we'd roll them in flour with a little salt and pepper and form them into patties for frying as you would with hamburger. We always enjoyed this dish!

—Juanita Reynolds Merritt, Joppa, Maryland

Potato Dumplings

Shared by Lori Grajek, Royal Oak, Michigan

2 pounds potatoes
4 slices white bread
1 teaspoon salt
1/4 teaspoon pepper
1 onion, grated
1 teaspoon minced parsley
2 eggs, beaten
1/4 cup flour
1-1/2 quarts boiling salted water

Wash, peel and grate raw potatoes. Using cheesecloth, squeeze as much starch out of the potatoes as possible. Soak bread in a little cold water. Squeeze as much water out of the bread as possible. Mix bread, salt, pepper, onion and parsley. Add potatoes and beaten eggs and mix well. Form mixture into balls. Roll them lightly in flour. Drop into salted boiling water (1 teaspoon salt for each quart of water). Cover pot tightly and boil 15 minutes. **Yield:** 4 servings.

Chowchow Was Tasty End-of-Season Dish

WHEN THE FROST *was on its way, we'd pick everything left in our garden, chop it up together and pickle it to make a dish called Chowchow.*

We ate it on top of pinto beans. Chowchow could include green tomatoes, peppers, onions—anything you could find in the garden that the frost would kill.

Often, we added cabbage to Chowchow. Before we had refrigeration, we dug a large hole in the ground, lined it with tar paper, dry grass or hay and filled it with heads of cabbage. We'd put a lid on top and then cover it with dirt—the cabbage would keep for months!

—E.A. Amick, Greensboro, North Carolina

❀ German-Style Green Beans ❀

Shared by Dorothy Harrington, Caro, Michigan

I WAS 8 years old in 1930 and our family lived on a farm in Michigan.

We always had a huge garden—probably an acre or two—and we had lots to eat. Mother canned nearly 1,500 quarts of fruits, vegetables, meat, jams and more each year.

We grew lots of strawberries, raspberries, rhubarb, currants and elderberries. We also had a mulberry tree.

Pumpkins and squash grew at one end of our cornfield away from the sweet corn. My favorite vegetables were onions, lettuce, peas, carrots, red beets and green beans—which Mom used to make her German-Style Green Beans.

The muskrats usually managed to find the garden, but we always planted a little extra for them.

2 to 3 slices bacon, cut in 1/2-inch pieces
3 tablespoons onion, chopped
2 cups green beans, cooked
2 tablespoons vinegar
1 tablespoon sugar

Fry bacon until crisp. Drain and save 1 tablespoon of drippings in skillet. Saute onions until tender. Add green beans, vinegar and sugar. Cover and cook over medium heat until heated through, stirring occasionally. **Yield:** 3 to 4 servings.

❦ Sweet Potato Casserole ❦

Shared by Edward Fenning, Cherry Hill, New Jersey

GOOD COOKS don't always have to follow a written recipe and my mother was proof of that.

After she passed away, the recipe for her delicious clam chowder could not be found. The lamb-and-beef stew that our uncle enjoyed so much remained a mystery. So did the lentil soup with dumplings that she made from scratch.

Her recipes for baked ham with homemade stuffing, rice and bread puddings, lemon meringue pie and many other dishes are only memories since they were never written down.

Though she didn't commit all her recipes to paper, Mom did write down a few which she kept in an old tin box. One of my brothers found the box later and copied the recipes so we all could make the dishes Mom cooked for us through the Great Depression.

I still remember those great meals, which often included Mom's Sweet Potato Casserole. On Sundays, we'd have an extra-big feast and Mom always baked two pies. She vowed we were going to eat only one, but she'd never fail to offer us a second piece and soon the other pie was gone too!

6 sweet potatoes, cooked and sliced
8 tablespoons brown sugar, *divided*
5 tablespoons butter, *divided*
2 oranges
1/4 cup strained honey
1/2 cup orange juice
1/4 cup bread crumbs

In greased casserole, arrange a layer of sliced sweet potatoes. Sprinkle with 6 tablespoons brown sugar. Dot with 4 tablespoons butter and cover with a layer of thinly sliced, unpeeled oranges. Repeat layers. Mix orange juice and honey and pour over top. Combine bread crumbs with remaining 2 tablespoons brown sugar and 1 tablespoon butter and sprinkle over top. Cover casserole and bake at 350° for 30 to 40 minutes, removing cover for the last 15 minutes.

✺ Festive Salad with Celery Root ✺

Shared by Robert Trumeter, LaVerne, California

2 cups cooked celery root, diced
1 large onion, chopped
1 16-ounce can carrots, drained and diced
1 16-ounce can beets, drained and diced
3 to 4 large sweet pickles, chopped, optional
2 to 3 tablespoons oil
1/4 cup vinegar
1/4 cup sugar
1/2 teaspoon salt

In a large bowl, mix celery root, onion, carrots and pickles, if desired. In a small bowl, blend the oil, vinegar, sugar and salt. Add more sugar or vinegar if desired. Add to vegetable mixture and blend well. Just before serving, add diced beets and blend well. Note: Beets will color salad if added too far ahead of serving. As a substitute for celery root, cook a turnip and 2 or 3 arms of celery to make 1-1/2 to 2 cups.

'Leather Britches' Were Tasty Family Favorite

I GREW UP in the hills of West Virginia with nine brothers and sisters during the Depression. One vegetable dish our family especially enjoyed in winter was a big iron pot of "leather britches".

During summer, we'd help our mother can and pickle string beans to use all year long. Then, we'd clean the remaining beans, string them on coarse thread and hang them on a nail behind the stove.

Once those beans were dry as crisp twigs, we'd store them in white cloth flour sacks. Before Mother cooked them, she'd soak them overnight and it was hard to believe those dried-up beans could fill up her big iron kettle!

Cooked with a piece of ham, those "leather britches" made a tasty (and chewy) dish that the whole family loved.

—Edna Smith, Reisterstown, Maryland

Great-Grandma Trostle's Fruit Salad (with Dressing)

Shared by Patricia Spiegle, Grove, Oklahoma

WHEN I was growing up in Topeka, Kansas in the mid-'30s, my folks rented a large rooming house and boarded live-in guests to make some extra money.

We had a lot of ground meat casseroles or boiled dinners, since these dishes could be stretched. The one I remember most was Mom's Washday Boiled Dinner. It had a wonderful aroma as it simmered on the stove for hours.

When my younger brother and I got home from school, we were put to work preparing the fruit for Great-Grandma Trostle's Fruit Salad. It was a favorite in our family and a recipe that she handed down from her Pennsylvania Dutch heritage. We also feasted on my Godmother Alberta's Easy No-Fail Brownies and Aunt Cece's Hominy Corn Bread.

Each of us kids helped set the long dining room table and by the time Dad and the boarders arrived, supper was ready to be served. It all went like clockwork.

When my husband and I were raising our own family of six children, this special meal—filled with family memories—became their favorite, too.

3 large naval oranges, peeled, sectioned and white membrane removed
3 large Delicious apples, peeled and quartered
1 cup canned chunk pineapple, drained, juice reserved
1 cup celery, stringed and diced
1 cup dates, seeded and chopped
3/4 cup raisins

In a salad bowl, combine the fruit, celery, dates and raisins. Top with cooled dressing and serve.

Fruit Dressing
1-1/2 cups pineapple juice
4-1/2 teaspoons lemon juice
3 egg yolks, well beaten
2-1/2 tablespoons sugar
1/2 teaspoon salt
1/4 teaspoon paprika

Heat lemon juice and pineapple juice in a small pan over low flame. In a small bowl, combine beaten egg yolks, sugar, salt and paprika. Add to fruit juice mixture slowly and stir constantly until it thickens and is smooth. Remove from stove and let cool before pouring over fruit salad. **Yield:** 12 to 13 servings.

What a value *this* is!
More than sliced pineapple
. . . . the *center slices* at
no extra cost

just the
center slices

Libby's
Hawaiian
Sliced
Pineapple

LIBBY'S *Sliced* Hawaiian Pineapple—every single can of it—brings you *just the center slices!* Not ordinary sliced pineapple, but just the slices that are loveliest in color, richest in flavor, most uniform in size and shape. Packed in a syrup of pure pineapple juice and cane sugar, they reach you with all their extra goodness held.

Yet they cost you no more! Insist on getting this extra value. Your grocer has Libby's Sliced Hawaiian Pineapple or he can get it for you easily.

Ask for C r u s h e d, *too*

Libby's *Crushed* Pineapple is tangy-sweet; luscious; most convenient for pies, puddings, shortcakes. And—for a quick salad—mix it with cottage cheese! Libby, M⊆Neill & Libby, Honolulu, Hawaii

{ *Center slices, packed in 4 different sized cans,* offer the economy of quantities most practical for you }

ONE OF THE EXTRA VALUES IN LIBBY'S FAMOUS 100 FOODS

Wilted Lettuce
(Summer Salad)

Shared by Phyllis Jordan, Marion, Ohio

Leaf lettuce
Green onion, chopped
Bacon, fried crisp
  1/4 cup water
  3/4 cup vinegar
Sugar to taste

Pick fresh lettuce from the garden and wash it thoroughly. Mix in green onion and set aside. Fry bacon until crisp, then crumble and set aside. Combine water, vinegar and sugar. Stir into hot bacon grease and heat. Pour the heated mixture over lettuce and toss. Sprinkle crumbled bacon on top.

Mother Knew Importance of the Basic Food Groups

MY MOTHER *knew how important the basic food groups were long before they were popular. She always made tasty and nutritious meals for our family living in West Virginia during the Depression.*

Each time she opened jars or cans of vegetables, she saved the liquid. Every few days she made vegetable soup using it as a soup base and adding rice, vegetables and some meat stock. She knew back then that throwing away the leftovers from cooking vegetables meant losing a lot of vitamins.

She did the same thing with fruits—saving the juice—and used what she saved to make fruit drinks or thickened it and poured it over cobblers and cakes. —Margaret Faverty, Mapleton, Iowa

Chapter 2

Soups

Soups were an inexpensive way to feed
the family with beans, leftover meat and
homegrown vegetables.

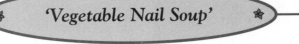

'Vegetable Nail Soup'

Shared by Barbara Iams Griffith, Helena, Montana

MY DAD *was a creative, playful man who always found ways to make us laugh. I remember so well one day when Mama made vegetable soup.*

My mother never shopped for soup ingredients. She made soup when she'd saved enough bones and meat scraps. When the pickings were slim, she'd brown the bones to make the broth look darker and richer than it was.

I must have been the one to complain about the thin soup that memorable evening. Daddy took control of the situation saying, "Plain old vegetable soup? We gotta do something about this!" Off he went, picking up small articles, shaking his head and putting them back down again. He made a big show of searching for that special item. Finally, he made his selection.

He headed back to the soup kettle that was simmering on the coal range, leaned over it and solemnly dropped in a long finishing nail. Muttering some "magic words", he gave the soup a few exaggerated stirs, straightened up and said, "Now we got soup!"

That night, we sat down happily to our buttered bread and bowls of thin "Vegetable Nail Soup".

Beef bones, leftover meat scraps,
  roast chicken carcass *or* any
  combination of these items
  4 cups cold water
Dash pepper
  1 teaspoon salt
  1 tablespoon parsley flakes,
    optional
  1 bay leaf, optional
  1 tablespoon *each* carrot,
    onion and celery, chopped
  1 carrot, chopped
  1 small onion, chopped

1 pint tomatoes, home-
  canned
1 tablespoon rice *or* pearl
  barley (soak barley first)

In a large pot, combine the first 7 ingredients. Cover and simmer slowly for 2 to 3 hours. Strain. Return meat pieces to the broth. Add remaining ingredients and simmer until vegetables are soft and rice or barley is done. If used, remove bay leaf and serve.

Lima Bean Soup

Shared by Mrs. Howard Schrenk, Ridgewood, New Jersey

1 pound dried lima beans
2 quarts water
2 large onions, chopped
2 stalks celery, chopped
2 carrots, chopped
2 tomatoes, peeled, seeded
   and chopped *or* 1 16-ounce
   can chopped tomatoes
3 tablespoons olive oil
3 peppercorns
1 bay leaf
Salt
Freshly ground black pepper
1/2 pound mozzarella cheese,
   cut into 1/2-inch cubes

Tabasco, optional
Scallion greens, chopped

Soak lima beans overnight. Drain. In a large kettle, combine water, beans, onions, celery, carrots, tomatoes, oil, peppercorns and bay leaf. Bring to a boil, cover and simmer for 45 minutes or until beans are tender. Remove from heat. Add salt and pepper to taste. Toss the cheese into the soup and when melted, serve soup in bowls. Sprinkle with Tabasco, if desired, and garnish with scallion greens.

Vegetable Soup Moved Sister to Tears

I WAS 3 years old when the Depression hit and my sister was 7. Like many people who had big gardens, my mother canned all kinds of foods, especially homemade vegetable soup.

By the end of the winter, we had mostly vegetable soup left in the cellar and every time my mother would go down there to get a jar for supper my sister would start to cry. She was so tired of it!

Though we did wish for more variety now and then, we knew we were lucky to be able to grow our own food.

—Joanne Hendrickson, Ankeny, Iowa

WPA Soup

Shared by Mary Kroos, Mason, Michigan

6 quarts water
2 cups celery, chopped
2 cups onions, chopped
2 cups potatoes, chopped
2 cups salami *or* summer
   sausage, cut into chunks
2 to 3 tablespoons butter
Salt and pepper
2 eggs, whipped

In a large pot, bring water to a boil.

Add all ingredients except eggs and simmer for 1 hour. Blend in whipped eggs and boil for 1 minute. Let soup chill 8 hours or overnight to enhance flavor. Heat and serve.

Green Bean Soup

Shared by Agnes Schussman, De Pere, Wisconsin

1 quart green beans, cut
   into 1-inch pieces
1 to 2 cups carrots and
   potatoes
Onion
Winter celery
Salt and pepper to taste
3 tablespoons vinegar
1/4 teaspoon sugar

2 tablespoons flour, browned
Shortening
Dash cinnamon

Combine first 5 ingredients and cook until tender. Add vinegar, sugar and cinnamon. Make a gravy of flour and shortening and add it to soup.

Depression Cabbage Soup

Shared by Betty Gusler, Zeeland, Michigan

4 cups cabbage, coarsely chopped
1 cup potatoes, chopped
3 cups water
1 cup sweet onion, chopped
2 tablespoons butter *or* margarine
2 slices bacon

Salt and pepper
2 tablespoons cornstarch
1 cup milk

Combine first 7 ingredients and cook until tender. Dissolve cornstarch in milk and stir into soup. Cook until thickened.

Salmon Soup

Shared by Mrs. Roscoe Gallivan, Columbia, Missouri

BACK IN THE *early 1930s, my family enjoyed plenty of hot bowls of Salmon Soup on cold winter evenings. It was one of my father's favorites.*

Mom would serve it with crackers or, for a special treat, with toast. Our vegetable would be a dish of home-canned tomatoes and for dessert we might have a piece of one-egg cake and a bowl of fruit or berries.

They were simple meals, but they got us through tough times.

1 small can salmon, flaked
1 quart milk *or* 1 small can milk, diluted
1 tablespoon butter *or* oleo
1 tablespoon flour, optional
1 tablespoon onion, finely chopped, optional

Prepare salmon. Warm milk over low heat. Do not boil. Thicken mixture with 1 tablespoon flour, if desired. Stir in salmon and butter. Add onion, if desired. Heat and serve at once with crackers or toast.

Ox Tail Soup

Shared by David Dickey, Upland, Indiana

MY FARMER *parents were married during the Great Depression, and my earliest memories are of sharing their joy in eating the food they grew themselves.*

No one had any money, so most goods and services were traded. My dad was a talented butcher, and for turning a cow into four quarters of beef, his fee was "the head, the heart, the hide and the tail".

He sold the hide to a tannery for cash which he used to buy the basics—salt, sugar and flour. He traded the head and the heart to neighbors for their more "exotic" vegetables like celery and turnips. We grew onions, carrots and potatoes.

The tail was the basis for my mom's Ox Tail Soup. In those days, butchering tended to be an event and the neighbors knew about it. They also knew about Mom's Ox Tail Soup and frequently happened to find themselves in our yard at mealtime.

Mom or Dad would always invite them to stay for supper. At first they'd refuse, saying they didn't want to put us out. But after the second invitation, they were quick to accept since we'd "insisted". A few extra people always seemed to be at our table when we had Ox Tail Soup.

Beef tail
Salt and pepper
Water
Potatoes, peeled and cubed
Onions
Carrots
Celery, optional
Turnips, optional

Separate the skinned beef tail at the joints. Salt and pepper generously. Place in a large pot and cover with water. Bring to a boil and skim off fat and debris. Add vegetables and continue cooking until meat and vegetables are done and the meat has separated from the bone. Serve in bowls with plenty of homemade bread.

Pink Soup

Shared by Lillian Marcotte, Woodstock, Vermont

1-1/2 tablespoons butter
1-1/2 tablespoons flour
1-1/2 quarts milk
  1/2 teaspoon salt
  1/4 teaspoon nutmeg
    2 tablespoons beets, cooked, finely ground

In a double boiler, mix all ingredients and cook until thick.

Sourgrass Soup

Shared by Julia Kapinos, Norwich, Connecticut

1 pound sourgrass leaves
2 cups water
2 cups milk *or* 1 cup milk and 1 cup cream
2 tablespoons butter
Salt and pepper
4 potatoes, peeled, cooked

Rinse leaves, then place in pot with water. Boil until leaves are tender. Add milk and butter and simmer for 10 minutes. In saucepan, boil the potatoes, then set aside. In last 5 minutes of boiling soup, add the potatoes so that the fragrance and taste of the sourgrass leaves will seep into the potatoes. Add salt and pepper to taste.

Summer at Grandma's Meant
Homemade Tomato Soup

THE FOOD I remember most from the 1930s is the delicious tomato soup that my grandmother made when we spent the summers with her in Alabama.

She'd open a jar of tomatoes she'd canned from her summer crop, season it with a little salt and pepper and add cornmeal for thickening.

Grandma's tomato soup—served hot or cold—was a meal we all loved! —Mrs. Harold Little, Memphis, Tennessee

Tomato Soup

Shared by Lillian Flanum, Clear Lake, Wisconsin

1 quart tomatoes, home-
   canned *or* freshly cooked
1/4 cup onion, chopped
1 teaspoon salt
Pepper to taste
2 tablespoons butter
2 quarts milk
1/4 teaspoon baking soda

Heat tomatoes, onion, salt, pepper and butter together and let simmer until blended. Add the baking soda and stir. Bring mixture to a boil, then reduce heat. In the meantime, heat the milk in a larger kettle that will hold all of the ingredients. Just before milk starts to boil, turn heat off and slowly pour the tomato mixture into the milk, stirring constantly.

Chicken Corn Soup

Shared by Helen Heiland, Joliet, Illinois

6 cups chicken broth, seasoned
2 cups chicken
2 cups corn kernels, cut off cob
1 cup homemade noodles, broken into 1-inch pieces
1 cup celery, chopped
2 tablespoons parsley, chopped
1 teaspoon salt
1/4 teaspoon pepper, freshly ground
Hard-boiled eggs, optional

Cook chicken in the broth until tender. Remove from broth, skin and cut into bite-size pieces. Bring the broth to a boil and add corn, noodles, celery, parsley, salt and pepper. Boil for 5 minutes and add chicken. Garnish with slices of hard-boiled eggs.

Milk Bean Soup

Shared by Mrs. Robert Markey, York, Pennsylvania

1 pound dry pea beans
Water
1 teaspoon salt
Milk
Bread, cubed
Butter
Salt to taste

Cook pea beans in salted water until soft. Add milk to mixture to form desired consistency. Add a little butter and salt to taste. Use purchased or homemade bread cubes. Place on a cookie sheet and pour melted butter over cubes. Toast cubes under the broiler. Serve in a separate bowl and add to soup as desired.

Shared by E. Cameron, Seattle, Washington

I WAS A YOUNG girl during the Depression and I remember those years, and the accompanying droughts, very vividly. But I don't remember ever going hungry on our North Dakota farm.

We'd heard that people in the western part of the state were much worse off than we were, since no crops or gardens would grow because of the drought.

One evening our family visited another farm family in the area. As the men were still doing their chores, the lady of the house was preparing the evening meal—Poor Man's Soup. It was something my mother had never made, so I asked for the recipe. We all enjoyed it very much and it became one of my husband and family's favorites in later years. I still enjoy making it and prefer it to today's potato soup recipes.

    2 **large onions, chopped**
Water
    6 **large white potatoes,**
        peeled, cut into chunks
Milk
Bacon, fried, crumbled,
  optional
Ham cubes, optional
Salt and pepper

In a saucepan, combine onions and 1-1/2 inches of water. Place potatoes over onions. Boil until tender but not mushy. Mash with potato masher, leaving chunks of potatoes not thoroughly crushed. Add milk to make a thick soup consistency and heat. Do not boil. If desired, crumble crisp bacon over the top of each bowl of soup or add cubes of ham to the pot of soup. Salt and pepper to taste.

Cream of Spinach Soup

Shared by Winnie Malone, Westerville, Ohio

1/2 pound fresh spinach
1 quart liquid, combination of milk and spinach water
4 tablespoons flour
1-1/2 teaspoons salt
1/8 teaspoon pepper
4 tablespoons butter *or* bacon fat

Wash spinach carefully in warm water and put in a saucepan. Do not add water. Place on stove. Stir until spinach becomes wilted. Continue to cook until the leaves are tender, about 15 to 20 minutes. Drain moisture from leaves and save. Chop the spinach leaves finely. Pour water from cooking spinach into a quart measure. Add enough milk to make 1 quart. Make a sauce with remaining ingredients and the milk mixture. Add spinach. Heat through and serve.

Lettuce or Spinach Soup

Shared by Dena Dikin, Fraser, Michigan

1/2 cup onion, chopped
1/4 cup flour, slightly browned
4 cups water
1 large head lettuce *or* spinach, washed, cut up
2 garlic cloves, finely chopped
1/2 cup sour cream

In a Dutch oven, saute the onion. Stir in flour and garlic. Add water and bring to a boil. Add lettuce or spinach. Boil 15 to 20 minutes. Remove from heat. In a small bowl, beat together 2 tablespoons of hot soup and the sour cream. Blend into soup and serve. If you don't have sour cream, beat together 1 egg, 1/4 cup vinegar and 2 tablespoons of hot soup. Blend into soup and serve.

Doggie Soup

Shared by Doris Wagner, Lancaster, Pennsylvania

2 pounds hot dogs, diced
5 pounds potatoes, diced
1 stalk celery, diced
1 medium onion, diced
1 bay leaf
Salt and pepper to taste

Put above ingredients in a pot and cover with water. Heat to boiling.

Rivels (Dumplings)
5 eggs
1/2 eggshell water
1/2 teaspoon salt
2 cups flour

Beat eggs, water and salt. Add flour a little at a time. Mix dough until it's stiff. Immediately drop by quar-ter-teaspoonfuls into the boiling soup. Cook about 20 to 25 minutes until potatoes and rivels are done. Remove bay leaf and serve.

Winter Soup

Shared by Alice Campbell, South Sioux City, Nebraska

1 quart canned beef, including broth
1 quart tomatoes
1 quart green beans
1 to 2-1/2 cups potatoes, boiled
1 to 1-1/2 cups cut corn
Salt and pepper

Simmer first 5 ingredients together until hot. Season to taste with salt and pepper.

Mom's Farina Soup

Shared by Margaret Pache, Mesa, Arizona

1 onion, finely chopped
4 tablespoons oil
1 teaspoon salt
1 pound veal, cubed
3 carrots, diced
1 kohlrabi, diced
2 medium potatoes, diced
3 parsley roots and greens
2 quarts water

Brown onion in oil about 5 minutes. Add salt and veal. Cover and simmer for 25 minutes, adding small amounts of water if needed. Add carrots, kohlrabi, potatoes and water. Tie parsley greens with a string and add to soup. Simmer about 1 hour or until vegetables are tender. Remove tied parsley.

Farina Dumplings
   1 egg, *separated*
  1/2 cup farina
Dash salt

Beat egg white until stiff. Fold in egg yolk, farina and dash of salt. Make a stiff paste. Drop farina dumplings by teaspoonfuls into boiling soup. Simmer 15 minutes.

Old-Fashioned Coffee Soup Made Special Snack

WHEN WE RAN SHORT *of milk during the Depression years, Mother would serve Coffee Soup, which was bread torn in pieces with hot coffee and sugar in a bowl. If we had milk, we had the bread and sugar in a bowl with milk.*

I liked Coffee Soup then, and I still eat it as a snack today. So do my six grown children and some of my grandchildren! We especially enjoy it with home-baked bread.
        —Norma Bertolette, Washingtonville, Ohio

Creamed Green Bean And Potato Soup

Shared by Mike Beliak, Las Vegas, Nevada

1   **pound green beans**
Water
2   **teaspoons salt**
1   **large potato, cubed**
2   **tablespoons flour**
8   **ounces sour cream**
1/4 **cup vinegar *or* more to**
      taste

Wash beans and remove ends and strings. Place in pot and cover with water. Add salt. Cook, covered, for approximately 30 minutes or more, adding potato during last 10 to 15 minutes of cooking. (More water may be added if needed.) Let cool. Mix flour with sour cream and add to cooked beans, stirring thoroughly. Stir in vinegar (could make liquid curdle). Return to heat and simmer until hot. Do not bring to a boil.

Broken Pretzels Were Key to Special Soup

I RECALL one Depression-era dish that really hit the spot on cold snowy days.

We lived in the Lebanon Valley of Pennsylvania where there were numerous pretzel bakeries. They sold broken pretzels at a much-reduced price.

Mother would fill a deep bowl with broken pretzels, then heat a pot of milk almost to boiling. She'd add a pat of butter and pepper to the bowl, then pour the hot milk on top of the pretzels.

Next, she'd put a plate over the top of the steaming bowl until the pretzels softened—what a great way to warm up!

Even now, cool winter mornings sometimes awaken that memory and I make a bowl of pretzel soup.

—Russell Kreider, Vero Beach, Florida

Dad's Bean Soup

Shared by Mona Blanchard, Presque Isle, Maine

ONE OF MY *father's jobs was cooking for the men who worked in the lumber camps. Both he and my mother were very good cooks and Dad's Bean Soup was one of our favorite meals during the Depression.*

I was born in 1932, one of 12 children, and I can remember some hard times during those years. I learned to cook at a very young age and this soup was one meal that helped get us through.

I now have four children of my own and five grandchildren. Often when we get together, we include this old family favorite on the menu.

2 **cups white pea beans, washed**
1 **medium onion, diced**
Salt and pepper to taste
2 **tablespoons butter** or **margarine**
4 **cups water (you may need to add more)**
1 **small can milk**
1 **cup cream**

1 to 1-1/2 quarts milk

Put first 5 ingredients in a 2- to 3-quart Dutch oven. Bring to a boil, then reduce heat to medium. Cook until beans are done. The liquid should be cooked down. Do not drain. Add canned milk to the liquid. Then add cream and 1 to 1-1/2 quarts milk.

Depression Soup

Shared by Gilbert Golla, Grand Rapids, Minnesota

1/3 **cup ketchup**
2/3 **cup boiling water**

Combine in a mug, stir and you have Depression Soup.

Grandma Schroth's Lentil Soup

Shared by Susan Jansen, Smyrna, Georgia

- 2 packages lentils
- 4 large carrots
- 4 stalks celery
- 1 medium onion
- 1 medium potato
- 1/4 to 1/2 pound country ham pieces *or* 1 large ham shank with bone
- 8 to 9 cups water

Salt and pepper

Sort through lentils, then rinse well in colander. Finely chop all vegetables. (I recommend chopping them separately in a food processor.) Combine all ingredients in a pot with water. Bring to a boil, then turn stove to low and simmer for 5 to 6 hours uncovered, stirring occasionally. Add salt and pepper to taste. Fat will rise to the top. Skim off and, if necessary, add water to reach desired consistency. Soup will thicken by itself. **Yield:** A lot. Great for freezing and using through the winter.

Mother's Homemade Potato Soup

Shared by Patsy Ann Penny, Malvern, Arkansas

- 5 to 6 medium potatoes, cut in small chunks
- 1 medium onion, chopped

Salt and pepper to taste
- 1 tablespoon parsley flakes
- 1/2 cup butter
- 1/2 cup milk

Combine potatoes, onion, salt, pepper and parsley flakes. Cook until potatoes are tender and turn burner off. Add butter and milk. Mix well. Serve with crackers or corn bread.

Old-Fashioned Vegetable Soup

Shared by Nellie Hicks, Eudora, Kansas

I GREW UP on a farm, and through the summer we enjoyed okra, cabbage, tomatoes, onions, lettuce, spinach and all kinds of vegetables from our garden. The winter months meant plenty of canned vegetables and fruit. We also dried fruit for making pies.

My mother, like most farm wives of her day, was always able to prepare meals from very little when our food supply ran low.

I still remember Mom's Old-Fashioned Vegetable Soup. It was delicious with homemade bread fresh from the wood-burning oven. Every summer, I can several quarts of this soup and enjoy the memories all winter long.

2 cups chicken broth
4 cups water
2 cups tomatoes, diced
1/4 cup celery, chopped
1/4 cup onion, chopped
1 tablespoon salt
1 teaspoon pepper
2 teaspoons Worcestershire sauce
1/4 teaspoon chili powder
2 bay leaves

1 cup carrots, sliced
1 cup potatoes, diced
1 cup cabbage, chopped
1/2 cup okra, sliced
1/2 cup corn
2 garlic cloves
1/2 cup peas

Combine ingredients in soup kettle. Cover and simmer about 45 minutes. **Yield:** 8 servings.

50

Potato and Turnip Stew

Shared by Eunice Sharp, Beloit, Wisconsin

I WAS 8 YEARS OLD when the Depression hit. At that time, most cooking was done by the "dumping" method rather than following written recipes. I often watched my mom make cakes by adding ingredients until the mixture looked and felt right.

Mom was also good at getting the most out of food. Whenever we got bacon—no matter how much or how little—she'd cut the package in half to make it go further.

It was always a treat to get bacon because that meant we might have Mom's Potato and Turnip Stew. It was easy to make and very filling.

2 to 3 strips bacon, cut into 1-inch pieces
1/2 turnip, peeled and cut into 1-inch cubes
Water
Potatoes, peeled and quartered
Salt and pepper to taste

Fry bacon until grease starts to show on bottom of pan. Add turnip and enough water to cover. Cook on high while peeling potatoes. Stir in potatoes and add more water if needed to cover. Salt to taste. When potatoes and turnips are tender, pepper to taste.

Milk-Noodle Soup

Shared by Florence Dean, Towson, Maryland

1 quart whole milk
1-1/2 cups noodles, uncooked
1 square (1 inch) butter
Salt and pepper to taste

Heat milk slowly and bring to a boil. Add uncooked noodles. Cook until tender, about 5 minutes. Add butter, salt and pepper. **Yield:** 4 servings.

Homemade Chicken Soup

Shared by Sarah Curci, San Jose, California

3 quarts water
1 whole chicken (washed thoroughly, insides removed)
1 onion, quartered
4 medium celery stalks
2 chicken bouillon cubes
2 sprigs parsley
1 teaspoon salt
1/2 teaspoon garlic powder *or* 1 whole fresh garlic clove
1/2 cup parsley, chopped
1/2 cup carrots, thinly sliced
1 to 2 drops yellow food coloring, optional

Using a deep soup pot, submerge whole chicken in water. Add onion, celery, bouillon, parsley sprigs, salt and garlic powder. Cook all together for 1 hour until chicken is tender. Turn heat off and remove whole chicken from soup pot. Let cool. Strain soup into clean pot. Press onion and celery gently to extract all flavor when pouring through strainer. Put soup pot back on stove to boil. Add carrots and cook until carrots are tender. Skin and bone chicken, using only the best part of the chicken. Cut chicken into large meaty chunks. Add chicken and chopped parsley to soup. Do not bring to a boil after adding meat, otherwise chicken could become stringy and tough. Add food coloring, if desired.

❧ Wild Mustang Grape Soup ❧

Shared by Lynette Pittsford, Austin, Texas

MY FAMILY lived on a ranch in Texas during the Depression years. I'll always remember my dad gathering wild mustang grapes in August and September.

We boiled them and strained them through white cloth. Then we put the beautifully colored juice in bottles and capped them with a hand-operated bottle-capper.

During the cold winter months, my mother made Wild Mustang Grape Soup for breakfast. We ate it with a slice of homemade bread and butter and we all loved it!

> 2 **cups water**
> 1/3 **cup grape juice**
> **Sugar to taste**
> **Flour**

Combine water and grape juice and heat. Add sugar to taste. Stir in flour to reach desired consistency.

❧ Different Bean Soup ❧

Shared by Grace Wismer, Titusville, Pennsylvania

> 2-1/4 **cups navy beans**
> 2 **quarts water**
> 1 **to 1-1/2 pounds smoked ham steak *or* shoulder *or* hocks**
> 1 **cup onion, chopped**
> 1 **cup celery, chopped**
> 1/4 **teaspoon pepper**
> 1 **teaspoon nutmeg**
> 1 **teaspoon oregano**
> 1 **teaspoon basil**
> 1 **teaspoon salt**

Soak beans overnight. Drain. Combine beans, water and ham in large kettle. Simmer covered for 1-1/2 hours. Remove 1 cup beans. Place beans in a small bowl and mash well. Remove ham and trim meat from bone. Cut ham into pieces. Return mashed beans and ham to kettle. Stir in remaining ingredients. Simmer for 30 to 45 minutes or until beans are tender.

Mother Made Many Creative Soups

I WAS a little girl growing up in the big city during the Depression, so there was no garden to help out and no home canning.

But Mother was very resourceful at keeping us well-fed on what I now realize must have been very little money.

One of her economical tricks was to make a visit to the local butcher late Saturday afternoon and get a bundle of chicken feet.

She'd scald and skin them, then boil them for several hours with a bunch of soup greens. The feet were discarded and the broth became the foundation for a pot of soup—different every time—and for cooking rice or cereal.

Farina and coarse cracked wheat were very cheap and, when cooked in the broth, poured into a shallow pan and chilled, could be used many different ways. It could be cut in squares and fried for breakfast or as a side dish, or cut in cubes and dropped into soup like croutons.

Cold broth was jellied and was sometimes made into an aspic. It was nutritious and, as Mother said, "strengthening".

—Ellen Huckaby, Frankfort, Kentucky

❋ Old-Fashioned Tomato Soup ❋

Shared by Nathalie Levesque, Atholville, New Brunswick

1 19-ounce can tomatoes, cut into pieces
1 can water
1 onion, cut into pieces
1 cup milk
1/2 teaspoon baking soda

In a medium-size pot, mix tomatoes, water and onion. Bring mixture to a boil and let simmer for 5 minutes. Turn off heat. Add milk and baking soda, then serve.

Tramp Soup

Shared by Clara Troyer, Clymer, New York

1 **quart canned sausage** *or*
　　store-bought sausage
Water
Potatoes, sliced
　1 **small onion, cut up**
Milk
Salt and pepper

Pour grease off of canned sausage. If store-bought, fry and pour grease off. Cut into pieces. Combine sausage, water, potatoes and onion. Cook until tender. Add milk and bring to a boil. Salt and pepper to taste. Serve with crackers.

Onion-Tomato Soup

Shared by Phyllis Jordan, Marion, Ohio

2 **large sweet Spanish**
　　onions (about 6 cups)
1/2 **cup butter**
　2 **14-1/2-ounce cans stewed**
　　tomatoes
　3 **10-1/2-ounce cans beef**
　　broth
1/2 **teaspoon basil**
Salt and pepper to taste

Peel onions and slice thinly. In large saucepan, saute onion in but-ter. Add tomatoes, beef broth and spices. Cook over low heat for 45 minutes. Serve with toasted French bread.

Cabbage Soup

Shared by Tamara Costello, Dennis, Massachusetts

2 pounds fresh cabbage
2 carrots
2 stalks celery
1 celery knob
3 tomatoes *or* 1 tablespoon
 tomato puree
3 medium potatoes
3 tablespoons butter *or*
 bacon fat, *divided*
1 large onion, sliced
6 to 8 cups beef *or* chicken
 consomme
1 tablespoon flour
1/2 teaspoon salt
1 tablespoon parsley,
 minced
1 tablespoon dill, minced
1 cup sour cream

Cut cabbage into quarters, discarding the hard core and any hard ribs of the leaves. Pour boiling water over the cabbage to scald it. Rinse with cold water and set aside to drain well. Chop cabbage coarsely when drained. Cut the carrots and celery into 1-inch pieces. Cube the celery knob. Peel and seed the tomatoes. Cut the potatoes into halves. Add these vegetables (not the onion or cabbage) to the consomme and bring to a boil, then simmer gently. In another pot, simmer onion for 5 minutes in 2 tablespoons butter or bacon fat. Add the cabbage. Cover the pot and braise gently for 20 minutes. Add the consomme to this mixture a couple spoonfuls at a time and continue cooking for 30 minutes. The cabbage should become pinkish. Brown the flour in the remaining butter or bacon fat. Thicken the soup with this and add the salt, parsley and dill. Bring to a boil. Cook for 20 minutes. Serve sour cream at the table to be added, if desired.

Huckleberry Soup

Shared by Doris Angeloff, New Cumberland, Pennsylvania

DURING THE DEPRESSION *years, my grandfather would head out in the wee hours of the morning to pick huckleberries. When he came home, my mother would clean them and we would have this delicious Huckleberry Soup for supper. It was a real treat!*

Clean huckleberries
White bread, in bite-size pieces
Ice cubes
Milk
Sugar

Combine huckleberries, bread and ice cubes. Cover with milk. Each individual sweetens soup with sugar to his or her own taste.

Sugar's Indiana Chowder

Shared by Diane Watts, McLean, Virginia

2 tablespoons margarine *or* butter
1 large onion, chopped
1-1/2 pounds ground chuck *or* round
1 16-ounce can tomatoes
2 8-ounce cans tomato sauce
1 4-ounce jar pimentos, chopped
1/2 pound mushrooms
1 teaspoon salt
1 teaspoon pepper
1 teaspoon sugar
1 teaspoon garlic salt
12 ounces wide egg noodles

Melt margarine and saute onion until translucent. Break up ground beef and cook until just pink. Add tomatoes, tomato sauce, pimentos, mushrooms and spices. Bring to a boil and top with noodles. Cover and boil for 5 minutes. Reduce heat and simmer for 25 minutes. Stir. Let stand for about 15 minutes, then serve.

Milk Soup Was Smooth and Creamy Treat

I DON'T CHERISH *the memories of all the side pork and fried pota-toes we ate during the 1930s, but I did love my mother's recipe for Milk Soup.*

It was always hot and creamy with lots of butter floating on top, and little dumplings would form as the soup cooked. We ate a lot of this soup when we lived on our farm in Michigan, and I vividly remember the rich, smooth flavor. —Joann Jaeger, Chetek, Wisconsin

Sour Cream Vegetable Soup

Shared by Irene Dhein, Cleveland, Wisconsin

3 medium carrots, sliced
2 stalks celery, sliced
30 green *or* yellow beans
 (*or* both), cut into 1-inch
 pieces
2 kohlrabies, diced
1 medium onion, chopped
1 4-1/2-ounce can peas *or*
 1 cup fresh peas
2 medium potatoes, peeled
 and diced
1 cup sour cream, *divided*
2 tablespoons flour
1 tablespoon vinegar
3 tablespoons sugar
2 tablespoons butter
1 tablespoon salt
1/4 teaspoon pepper

Prepare all vegetables except peas and onion. Wash and drain. Pour hot water over and let stand a few minutes. Drain and put in soup kettle and cover with cold water. Add onion and boil until tender. Drain canned peas and add to cooked vegetables. (If using fresh, add them halfway into cooking time.) Mix flour into 1/2 cup sour cream. Add other 1/2 cup and blend until smooth. Take 1 ladle of hot liquid and pour slowly into cream mixture so it does not curdle. Add cream mixture to soup and keep stirring until soup boils. Add last 5 ingredients and stir. Heat through and serve.

Chapter 3

Breads and Biscuits

Flour, lard and a little creativity added up
to tasty, filling breads on the table.

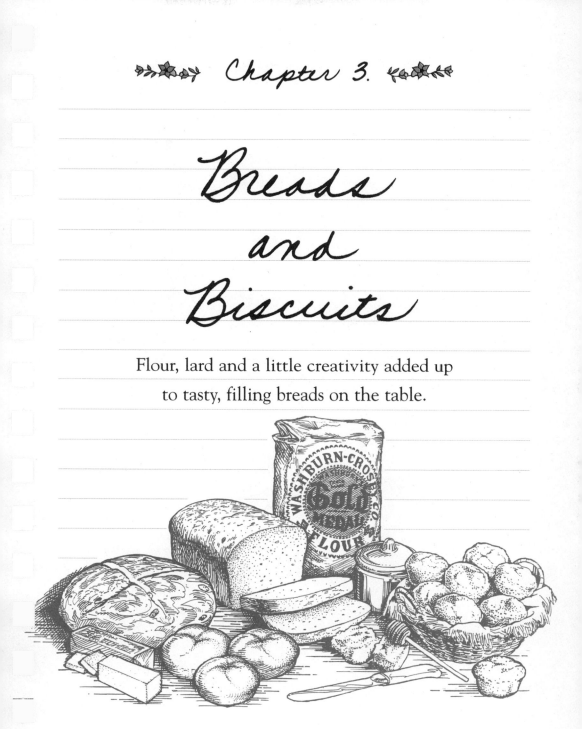

Corn Bread Tasted Too Good to Be 'Depression Food'

DURING *the Depression, my days were spent in the hayfields of Illinois where I poked wire and stacked bales. Cooking for the threshers was a great source of pride for the farm ladies in the area and they always tried to outdo each other.*

I still remember my favorite meal—fried chicken, mashed potatoes, green beans, "wilted" lettuce and corn bread. It was always served because corn bread was the one food all of us loved. One old rascal ate several pieces of cake with no icing and then remarked it was the best "corn bread" he'd ever eaten.

As a child, I enjoyed many evening meals that consisted of corn bread broken up in a glass of milk. It was so good that I didn't realize we were poor and couldn't afford anything else! —Foster Marlow
San Marcos, Texas

Old Reliable Corn Bread

Shared by Linda Provis, Fremont, California

1 cup yellow cornmeal
1 cup all-purpose flour
2 tablespoons baking powder
1 teaspoon salt
1/3 cup shortening, softened
1 cup milk
1 egg
1/2 to 1 cup sugar (optional)

Sift dry ingredients into mixing bowl. Cut in shortening until well blended. Beat milk and egg together. Mix with dry ingredients until just blended. If desired, add 1/2 to 1 cup sugar to sweeten. Mix well. Pour into well-greased 8-inch square pan and bake at 400° for 25 minutes.

Dumplings

Shared by Dollie Deitrich, Mingoville, Pennsylvania

2 cups flour
4 teaspoons baking powder
1 teaspoon salt
2 tablespoons shortening
3/4 to 1 cup milk
Broth

Sift dry ingredients. Add shortening, then milk until thick batter is obtained. Drop by teaspoonfuls in boiling broth. Cover and cook 12 minutes. Be sure not to lift lid.

Corn Bread, Cornmeal Mush Are Treasured Recipes Today

OUR PARENTS lived through the Depression and we remember them telling us how corn bread, hominy and cornmeal mush were some of the foods they ate most often.

They had those things on the table so often that today they really don't care much for them. But our family still uses those recipes and cherishes them as special foods!

We often fry mush for our breakfast and we still cook hominy in large iron kettles the old-fashioned way. It's good with a little butter or mushroom soup added. We also serve beans or milk and applesauce with our corn bread. It's a treat we all enjoy. —Mrs. Petie E. A. Schwartz
Seymour, Missouri

Brown Bread

Shared by Virginia Fackler, Garrettsville, Ohio

GRANDMA'S brown bread was one of my favorite foods when I was growing up in Nelson, Ohio—especially during maple-syrup-making time.

When I was 6 and my brother was 10, we'd wait in front of our house for my great-uncle to come by with his sap sled.

The sled carried a big vat, but there was room enough for us to hitch a ride to the sugar house. The fragrant smell of the boiling maple syrup was out of this world. Of course, we always had a quart jar with us to fill.

When we got home, Mom would make our favorite brown bread from Grandma's special recipe. We loved it with our syrup!

2 **cups sour milk**
1 **cup maple syrup**
2 **cups graham flour**
1 **cup white flour**
2 **teaspoons baking soda**
1 **teaspoon baking powder**
2 **tablespoons oil**
Salt

Mix soda into sour milk and set aside for a few minutes. Mix remaining ingredients together and add sour milk mixture. Stir and put in pans. Bake at 350° for 1 hour. **Yield:** 2 loaves.

Homemade Biscuit Sandwiches Made Big Impression at Lunchtime

DURING THE DEPRESSION, our friends and neighbors talked a great deal about how hard times were, but our family didn't know the difference. We were mighty thankful for what we had.

I noticed other kids who had sandwich bread in their lunches, but I always had biscuit sandwiches filled with cheese, peanut butter or fried eggs.

Those biscuit sandwiches must have been better than I thought because several times, my schoolmates bought a sandwich from me at lunchtime for a nickel! —Walter Dillard, Clearwater, Florida

❧ Dried Fruit and Soda Bread ❧

Shared by Shirley Forest, Eau Claire, Wisconsin

  3 cups all-purpose flour
  6 ounces or 1-1/3 cups dried mixed fruit bits, chopped
  1 cup quick-cooking oats
1/3 cup sugar
  2 teaspoons baking soda
  1 teaspoon salt
  1 egg, lightly beaten
1/4 cup unsalted butter *or* margarine, melted
1-1/3 cups buttermilk

Combine flour, fruit, oats, sugar, baking soda and salt in a large bowl. Make well in center. In a small bowl, beat together egg, butter and buttermilk. Add to well and stir just until dry ingredients are moistened. Do not over-stir. Mixture should be lumpy. Turn dough into greased 2-quart oval baking dish. Bake in 400° oven for 30 minutes or until golden brown and loaf sounds hollow when tapped with finger. Serve immediately or cool completely. Store at room temperature in a tightly sealed container until ready to serve. Can be stored up to 1 week. **Yield:** 8 servings.

Mama Sheridan's Baking Powder Biscuits

Shared by Esther Sheridan Auer, West Bend, Wisconsin

6 cups flour
1/2 cup dry milk
1 tablespoon salt
8 teaspoons baking powder
1 tablespoon lard *or* shortening
Cold water

Cut in shortening to dry ingredients. Add enough cold water to mix. Roll on floured bread board until about 1 inch thick. Cut with a large cookie or biscuit cutter (a floured drinking glass will work). Place on a large cookie sheet. Dot each biscuit with a dab of shortening. Bake at 400° until golden brown on top and done.

Johnny Cakes (Easy Method)

Shared by Rosemary Claghorn, Keystone, Indiana

3 cups self-rising flour
Water
Oil

Add water to make a dough (consistency of biscuit dough). Roll out 1/4 inch thick on well-floured board. Cut into strips 2 inches wide by 6 inches long. Put enough oil into skillet to cover the bottom 1/4 inch. Heat the oil until it is hot. Fry the strips until brown on one side and turn and fry the other side. Second side will only brown the bubbles. Pile on a plate and serve. Good hot or cold.

Ire Hobber

Shared by Dolores Leathers, Boonville, Missouri

1 cup flour
2 eggs
Milk
Dash salt
Oil

Mix flour, eggs and enough milk to make consistency of pancake batter. Add a dash of salt. Pour immediately into a 10-inch skillet with about 1/2 inch hot oil or fat. It will curl up on the sides. Let cook until the bottom is lightly browned. Take care and turn it over in skillet. Let brown on this side. When done, remove from fire and cut into 1-inch squares in the skillet. Pour into serving bowl and serve as a side dish with cooked beans. **Yield:** 4 to 5 servings.

Grandma's Fried Bread Was Special Treat

MY GRANDMOTHER *always bought flour in 100-pound sacks and baked bread nearly every day during the Depression.*

On some days, we had fried bread with lard and bacon grease or brown sugar. Once in a while when I'm baking bread, I'll fry some and remember that favorite treat from my childhood.
—Sophie Tysma, Moline, Illinois

Hominy Corn Bread

Shared by Judy Robertson, Russell Springs, Kentucky

1 cup hominy
1 tablespoon shortening, melted
2 eggs, beaten
1 cup milk
1/2 cup cornmeal
1/2 teaspoon salt
1 teaspoon baking powder

Combine hominy, shortening, eggs and milk. Add cornmeal, salt and baking powder. Let stand 5 minutes. Add 1 tablespoon more of milk if desired. Pour into large well-oiled pan and bake at 425° for 35 minutes or until a rich golden brown. **Yield:** 6 servings.

Bread Dumplings

Shared by Mrs. J. Marshall, Port Richey, Florida

2 eggs
1/2 cup milk
1 teaspoon salt
3 cups flour, sifted
Pinch baking powder
4 slices white bread, cut into cubes
Salted boiling water

Beat eggs, milk and salt in a large mixing bowl. Sift together flour and baking powder and gradually add with a large spoon. The dough must be smooth and stiff enough to hold its shape. Stir in bread cubes. Have a wet clean towel ready. Shape the dough with wet hands until it is oblong. Roll in a towel and drop into a large kettle of salted boiling water. Boil covered for 45 minutes. Take out of water carefully. Remove the towel and slice the dumplings 1/2 inch thick. If not sliced immediately, the steam cannot escape and dumplings will be soggy and hard. Keep hot until ready to serve.

Homemade Bread

Shared by Ruth Miller, Shreve, Ohio

5 cups lukewarm water
2-1/2 tablespoons yeast
2/3 cup brown sugar
2 tablespoons salt
1 cup vegetable oil
3 cups wheat flour
11 cups white flour, *divided*
Margarine

Dissolve yeast in water. Add sugar, salt, oil, wheat flour and 4 cups white flour. Beat together until smooth. Mix in enough remaining flour to form a soft dough that cleans the bowl. Knead 8 to 10 minutes. Place in a greased bowl, turning once to grease top. Cover and let rise in a warm place until double (1 hour). Punch down and let rise until double (1/2 hour). Punch down and let rise until double (1/2 hour). Divide dough into 5 loaves and put into 4 greased loaf pans. (Reserve one loaf for Lollipops recipe below.) Grease tops with vegetable oil and prick with fork. Let rise until double (1/2 hour). Bake at 350° for 35 to 40 minutes or until golden brown. Remove from pans and grease tops with margarine.

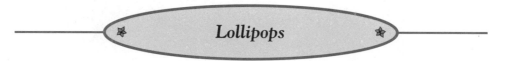

Lollipops

Shared by Ruth Miller, Shreve, Ohio

1 loaf bread dough (from above)
3/4 cup margarine
1-1/2 cups brown sugar
1 cup light cream

Melt margarine. Remove from heat. Add brown sugar and cream. Stir together. Return to heat and bring to a boil, stirring constantly. Pour into 9- x 13- x 2-inch pan. Divide dough into 15 balls and arrange on top of syrup mixture. Let rise in warm place for 20 minutes. Bake at 350° for 20 to 25 minutes. Serve while warm.

Mama's Old-Fashioned Butter Rolls

Shared by Grace Weeks, Kinston, Alabama

1 cup sugar
1 stick butter (more if
  needed)
Milk
Cinnamon, optional

Make up dough as you would for biscuits. Pinch out small amounts of dough. Roll out on floured cloth. Place a pat of butter on each and sprinkle generously with sugar. Roll each up and press ends together. Pick up carefully and place in deep baking dish, leaving a little space between each roll. Pour milk over rolls until they're covered. Sprinkle with remaining sugar (and cinnamon if you like). Bake for 45 minutes at 325°.

Mom's Homemade Bread Was Special After-School Snack

IN 1934, I was 5 years old and growing up on a farm north of Cozad, Nebraska. It was extremely hot that year, and a fine dust seemed to constantly settle over everything.

I walked down dusty roads about 1-1/4 miles to school. My Dad always said you could set your watch by my two dogs and my pet nanny goat. They'd trot out the gate and down the road to meet me at 4:00 every day when school was out.

While I was at school, Mother would bake homemade bread. It would still be warm from the oven when I got home, and a big slice of that bread with butter and some sugar sprinkled on top was a great treat!
—Bonnie Knuth, Lexington, Nebraska

Shared by June Crake, Grandville, Michigan

DURING the Depression, my parents raised sorghum cane and had it made into syrup. I remember taking the cane to a nearby farm and watching the mule go around and around to grind it, while the fire cooked the juices into sorghum syrup.

We didn't have much sugar during the '30s and Mother used the syrup to make her sweet molasses bread. I still enjoy making it just the way she taught me.

These days, my cousin in Iowa has begun growing sorghum again. He has the equipment to grind the cane by tractor instead of the old-fashioned way using a horse or mule. But the process is just as fascinating today as it was back then!

4 tablespoons lard *or* oleo
1/2 cup sugar
1 cup buttermilk *or* sour milk
1/2 cup molasses *or* sorghum syrup
1 teaspoon baking soda
1 teaspoon cinnamon
1/2 teaspoon nutmeg
1/4 teaspoon cloves
1-3/4 to 2 cups flour
1/2 cup raisins (put a little of the flour over them)

Cream lard and sugar. Add milk and molasses. Next add dry ingredients and the raisins. Do not overmix as this is a quick bread. If desired, sprinkle with 1 tablespoon of sugar before baking. Bake at 350° for 30 to 40 minutes. Remove from pan. Slice and serve with butter.

Mom's Baking Day Meant Plenty of Fresh Bread

WE ALWAYS HAD lots of good homemade bread to eat during the
Depression years.

Biscuits were part of our breakfast every morning and on my
mother's baking day, she made two huge loaves of bread in her turkey
roaster. It was delicious with the butter, jelly, apple butter and fruit preserves that we made.

She also made pans and pans of light, fluffy rolls and at least one
pan of cinnamon rolls. Sometimes I can almost smell that comforting aroma today!   —Phyllis Jordan, Marion, Ohio

❀ Nana's Applesauce Bread ❀

Shared by Bobbie Sanderson, Santa Ana, California

1/2 cup white sugar
1/2 cup brown sugar
1 cup applesauce
1 teaspoon vanilla
1 teaspoon baking soda
1-1/2 teaspoons cinnamon
1/2 teaspoon nutmeg
1/2 teaspoon pumpkin pie
spice
1/2 cup butter
2 eggs
1/3 cup milk
2 cups all-purpose flour

1/2 teaspoon salt

Heat oven to 350°. Grease bottom
only of bread pan. In a very large
bowl, mix all ingredients well. Pour
into baking pan and bake for 60 to
65 minutes or until toothpick inserted in the center comes out
clean. Cool about 5 minutes and
remove from pan. Finish cooling on
wire rack. When cooled, wrap in
plastic wrap and store in icebox.
Yield: 1 loaf.

Buttermilk Biscuits

Shared by Peggy Ratliff, North Tazewell, Virginia

2 cups self-rising flour
1 teaspoon salt
1/4 cup buttermilk
1/4 cup water
1/4 cup mayonnaise
Butter, melted

Mix all ingredients together. Stir into a ball. Place dough on a floured surface and knead lightly. Roll out about 1/2 inch thick and cut with biscuit cutter. Place on a baking pan and bake at 450° for 10 minutes or until brown. Brush melted butter on top.

Date and Nut Bread

Shared by Margaret Kleinjan, Palmdale, California

1 teaspoon baking soda
1 cup hot water
1 cup dates, pitted and cut up fine
1 large tablespoon butter
1 egg, beaten
3/4 cup sugar
3/4 cup walnuts, chopped
1/4 teaspoon salt
1-1/2 cups flour

Mix baking soda and hot water and pour over dates. Add remaining ingredients and mix all together. Put in a loaf pan. Bake at 325° for 1 hour.

St. Joseph Bread

Shared by Maureen Bailey, Godfrey, Illinois

MY GRANDMOTHER *carries on a tradition that her parents brought over from Italy when they settled in the U.S.*

Each year on March 19, we celebrate St. Joseph's Day. To honor this patron saint, Grandma serves 13 different foods at a family meal.

One of my favorite parts of this special meal is Grandma's St. Joseph Bread. I'm sharing her recipe for others of Italian heritage (or anyone who loves delicious homemade bread!) to try in March...or any time of the year.

1-1/2 cups warm water
2 1/4-ounce packages dry
   yeast
2 tablespoons shortening
1 tablespoon sugar
1 tablespoon oil
2 teaspoons salt
4-1/2 cups flour, *divided*
1 egg, beaten
1/4 cup sesame seeds (optional)

In a small bowl combine water, yeast, shortening, sugar, oil and salt. Let stand 5 minutes. Put 2-1/2 cups flour in large mixing bowl and add liquid mixture. Beat until blended. Stir in as much of the remaining flour as you can mix with a spoon. Knead in the rest of the flour to make a moderately stiff dough which is smooth and elastic (about 6 to 8 minutes). Shape into a ball and place in lightly greased bowl. Turn once to grease surface. Cover and let rise in a warm place approximately 45 minutes to an hour. It will double in size. Punch down and divide into 6 equal parts. Cover and let rest 10 minutes. Roll each piece into a 12-inch rope. Braid three ropes together for a loaf of bread. Place each loaf on a greased baking sheet. Cover and let rise until doubled (about 30 to 40 minutes). Brush tops and sides with egg. Add sesame seeds if desired. Bake at 400° for 20 minutes or until crust is light brown. Cool on wire rack. **Yield:** 2 loaves.

Home-Style Corn Bread

Shared by Deloris Beland, Broken Bow, Nebraska

1 egg
3 tablespoons sugar
1 cup sour milk *or* buttermilk
4 tablespoons shortening,
  soft or melted
1 cup flour
2 teaspoons baking powder
1/2 teaspoon baking soda
1/2 teaspoon salt
1 cup cornmeal, yellow
  preferred

Place egg and sugar in mixing bowl and beat lightly. Add sour milk or buttermilk and shortening. Sift flour, baking powder, baking soda and salt together; then add cornmeal and mix with above liquid. If batter seems stiff, a little more milk may be added. Grease a 9- x 9-inch pan generously with fresh bacon or meat fryings and cover with thick sprinkling of cornmeal. Pour batter in pan and bake at 425° until nicely browned or about 25 minutes. You may omit the sugar and use less flour, increasing cornmeal in proportion. **Yield:** 4 to 6 generous servings.

Corn Bread

Shared by Yvonne Monsauret, Riverside, California

1-1/2 cups yellow cornmeal
1/2 cup wheat flour
1/4 cup brown sugar
1/2 teaspoon baking soda
1 teaspoon salt
1 cup raisins
1 egg
1-1/4 cups sour cream
1 cup milk
1/4 cup butter, melted

Mix together the cornmeal, flour, sugar, baking soda, salt and raisins. Place a tablespoon of butter in a heavy cast-iron skillet and put in the oven. In another bowl, beat together the egg, sour cream, milk and butter. Add this to first mixture and stir well. Pour into the hot skillet and bake at 400° for 30 minutes. Test with a toothpick for doneness.

Mother Made Biscuits by the Bowlful

MY MOTHER *made lots of thrifty dishes during the Depression, and she had an interesting way of making biscuits.*

Since she bought her flour in large sacks which were hard to handle, Mother poured a weekly supply of flour into a big crockery bowl. She kept it in the cupboard, covered with a clean dish towel.

She made biscuits by adding the other ingredients right on top of the bowlful of flour and mixing it all with her hands. She'd lift out the dough and put the remaining flour back in the cupboard for next time.

Once our cat found the cupboard door open and had a good time exploring that bowl. She came out with her face covered with flour. My mother was fit to be tied—she had to throw out that whole bowl of flour and she didn't like to waste anything! —Suzie Frazelle, Seaside, Oregon

Grandmother Spitler's Rich Biscuits

Shared by Virginia Elliott, Naples, Florida

2 cups all-purpose flour
1/2 teaspoon salt
2 tablespoons sugar
1 tablespoon baking powder
1/4 cup sweet butter
1/4 cup vegetable oil
1/2 cup milk
1/4 cup coffee cream

Sift all dry ingredients together. Cut in butter and oil together until mixture resembles coarse crumbs. Make a well and add the milk and cream. Stir quickly and lightly with a fork until it forms a lump. Turn onto a floured board. Knead very gently about 10 times. Roll or pat the dough out about 1/2 inch thick. Using a biscuit cutter dipped in flour, cut straight down through dough and lift carefully onto an ungreased baking sheet and bake at 450° for 12 to 15 minutes. Watch so they brown lightly but do not scorch. Should make 10 to 12 depending on cutter size. I like to use a small "cheese glass" which will give you 15 to 16 small biscuits.

Poor Man's Bread

Shared by Patsy Spires, Cheshire, Ohio

1 cup flour
1 teaspoon baking powder
Water

Stir in enough water to make batter and pour into greased skillet. This is best in an iron skillet. Fry until brown on each side like a pancake. Great served hot with homemade butter and jelly.

Butterhorns

Shared by Pam Lemke, Windsor, Wisconsin

I'LL ALWAYS HAVE a special place in my heart for a dear lady who lived upstairs from my family when I was a little girl.

Ruth treated me as if I were her own granddaughter and whenever I visited, she always had some kind of fresh-baked bread, cookies or pie cooling on the table.

But my favorite homemade treat was her delicious butterhorns. Whenever I think of Ruth, I remember the tempting aroma of those mouth-watering rolls...and the special friendship we shared.

1-1/2 **cups milk, scalded**
1 **cup shortening**
1/2 **cup sugar**
Dash salt
1 **teaspoon vanilla**
1/2 **teaspoon nutmeg**
3 **packages dry yeast**
1/3 **cup warm water**
3 **eggs**
5 **to 6 cups flour**

In a large bowl, combine all ingredients except flour. Mix thoroughly. Add 2 cups flour and blend thoroughly. Gradually add about 3 to 4 more cups flour until you can form a tight soft ball. Place dough in a greased bowl and let rise. Roll dough 1/4 inch thick into a circle on a floured board. Cut into pie-shaped pieces and roll starting at wide end. Place on greased pan and let rise about 2 hours. Bake at 375° for 10 to 12 minutes.

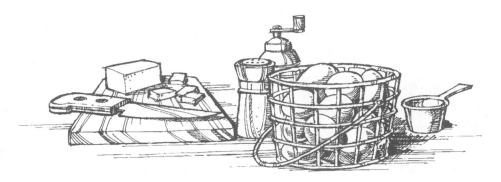

Sour Cream Tea Biscuits

Shared by Alice LaFrance, Blind Bay, British Columbia

2 cups flour
1 teaspoon white sugar
1/4 teaspoon salt
1/2 teaspoon baking soda
3 teaspoons baking powder
1/2 cup shortening
1 cup sour cream
3/4 cup cheddar cheese, grated

Preheat oven to 450°. Mix dry ingredients. Cut in shortening (until mixture resembles small peas). Add sour cream and cheese and blend thoroughly. Roll out dough and cut with cookie cutter. Place on ungreased pan. Bake for 12 minutes. Serve warm for best flavor.

Mama's Biscuit Recipe Required Special Touch

MAMA WORKED HARD keeping my dad, my two brothers and me fed during the Depression. Her garden pulled us through those times.

But I also remember the special way Mama made biscuits. First she'd sift flour into her shallow metal washpan. Then she'd make a well in the center of the flour and drop in a spoonful of baking powder, a bit of salt and some shortening scooped from the can.

After that, she'd start adding milk to the mixture until she was satisfied with the texture and amount. Then she'd turn the dough out onto the board, roll and cut it and bake the biscuits in a hot oven.

Though she never measured anything, her biscuits were always light and tasty. When I was old enough to bake them myself, I tried to get her to give me the exact measurements. But she insisted that it had to be done by feel and appearance. I've never been able to make biscuits that tasted as good as hers. —Beverly Allen, Coupeville, Washington

Dutch Oven Bread

Shared by Bernadine Kuchar, Roscommon, Michigan

2-1/2 cups warm water
    2 packages dry yeast
  1/2 cup sugar
  1/2 cup soft margarine *or*
      butter-flavored shortening
1-1/2 teaspoons salt
    7 cups flour
Milk

In a large bowl, mix thoroughly the water, yeast, sugar, margarine and salt. Let set 15 minutes until bubbly. Using a wooden spoon, add flour 1 cup at a time, stirring well before adding another. Turn on floured board or table and knead until elastic, adding flour if needed. Shape into a ball and put in a greased bowl. Grease top of dough lightly and cover. Let rise until double. Punch down. Place in 4- or 5-quart heavy round dutch oven pan. Let rise until double. Brush very lightly with milk and sprinkle flour all over top of bread. Bake at 325° for 65 to 70 minutes. (Place on lowest rack with upper rack removed. Bread could possibly get very high.) The last 20 minutes increase temperature to 400°. Remove and cool on wire rack.

White Bread

Shared by Betty Goss, Northbrook, Illinois

    1 cake yeast *or* 1/4-ounce envelope
1-1/2 quarts lukewarm milk (105-115°)
  18 cups white flour (16 cups is usually enough)
    1 egg
    2 tablespoons sugar
    1 tablespoon salt
    2 tablespoons shortening, melted
Butter

Dissolve yeast and sugar in 1 quart

lukewarm milk. (Use 2% or whole milk.) Add 6 cups of flour and beat well. Cover and let rise in warm place for 1-1/2 hours. Add rest of ingredients. Knead thoroughly. Place in greased bowl, cover and let rise 2 hours. Mold into 4 loaves and place in greased bread pans. Let rise 1 hour. Bake for 10 minutes at 350° and then 35 to 50 minutes at 300°. Turn out on racks, butter tops of loaves and cool. Can be wrapped in foil and frozen.

Raisin Bread

Shared by Linda Bruce, Haines, Alaska

MY GREAT-AUNTS *worked at the Sun-Maid raisin factory in California for nearly 50 years and my grandfather grew grapes on his ranch to harvest for raisins.*

When my brother and I spent summers with our aunts or on Grandpa's ranch, we were always treated to delicious dishes made with raisins.

Sometimes we couldn't wait for baking day and we'd run down the vineyard rows where large sheets of paper were spread on the ground full of grapes drying in the sun. We'd scoop up handfuls and stuff ourselves with the warm, sweet fruit.

As far back as I can remember, our aunts always had toasted Raisin Bread for breakfast—slathered with their homemade marmalade. It's an early-morning treat I'll never forget!

3 cups flour
1 teaspoon salt
3 teaspoons baking powder
1-1/2 tablespoons sugar
1 cup raisins, seeded
1-1/2 cups milk
2 tablespoons butter
1 egg, beaten

In a large bowl, combine the flour, salt, baking powder and sugar. Mix thoroughly. Add the remaining ingredients and mix well. Pour into greased loaf pan and bake at 350° for 50 minutes or until an inserted toothpick comes out clean. Remove from pan and cool on wire rack.

Gram's 'Handmade' Bread Got Us Through Tough Times

MY GRAM *was one of the best cooks in West Texas, even during the Depression when food was hard to come by.*

One of our favorites back then was Gram's Fried Corn Bread. She always had a coffee can of drippings on the back of the stove and she used them over and over.

When she made this bread, she'd put some drippings in her big iron skillet. While the skillet was getting to just the right temperature, she'd take some cornmeal and add enough boiling water to make a heavy paste.

Then she'd dip her palm into the heavy paste and pat it back and forth quickly since it was quite hot.

She'd make a platter of those patties, then drop them into the spattering drippings and fry them to a golden brown. Her Fried Corn Bread got us through many a day and it was good hot or cold as a snack!
—Helen Hillman
Prescott, Arizona

Zweiback or Top Hat Rolls

Shared by Evangeline F. Rew, Manassas, Virginia

1 package yeast
1 tablespoon sugar
2 tablespoons dry milk powder
1 teaspoon salt
2 tablespoons cooking oil
1-1/2 cups warm water
4 to 4-1/2 cups flour

Place all ingredients except flour in a bowl. Using a whisk, add 2 cups of flour and beat until smooth. Add 2 to 2-1/2 cups more flour and knead until smooth. Let rise until double. Knead down. Place rounded rolls of dough on greased pan. Make other balls of dough 1/2 size and place on top of larger ones. Poke down securely. Let rise. Bake at 400° for 12 minutes or until brown.

Dinner Rolls

Shared by Leona Mielke, Almena, Wisconsin

1-1/2 cups milk
1/2 cup shortening *or* margarine
1/3 cup sugar
2 teaspoons salt
1 large cake fresh yeast
1/2 cup lukewarm water
2 eggs, slightly beaten
6 to 7 cups flour

Heat milk until near boiling. Pour over shortening, sugar and salt in a large bowl. Cool to lukewarm. Then dissolve yeast in lukewarm water. Blend dissolved yeast and eggs into first mixture. Add 2 cups of flour and mix thoroughly. Stir in rest of the flour and knead until dough is smooth and elastic and does not stick to the board or bowl. Place in a greased bowl. Cover and let rise in a warm place until double. Shape or make into small balls. Let rise again until double. Bake 15 to 20 minutes at 350° until done.

Cornmeal Biscuits

Shared by Lucille Stamper, Danville, Indiana

1-1/2 cups flour
    3 teaspoons baking powder
    1 teaspoon salt
1/2 cup yellow cornmeal
1/4 cup shortening
3/4 cup milk

Sift together flour, baking powder and salt. Mix in the cornmeal and cut in the shortening until mixture looks like meal. Stir in milk to make a soft dough. Round up lightly on a floured board and knead. Roll out 1/4 inch thick. Cut and place on ungreased baking sheet. Place biscuits close together for soft sides or 1 inch apart for crusty sides. Bake 12-15 minutes at 425° until golden brown. **Yield:** 12 biscuits.

Egg Bread

Shared by Mrs. Horace Hancock, Abbeville, Alabama

2 cups cornmeal (fine)
1/2 teaspoon baking soda
    2 cups buttermilk
    1 teaspoon salt
    3 eggs

Mix all ingredients together well and pour into greased iron skillet.

Bake at 400° for 25 to 30 minutes or until golden brown. Serve with butter and buttermilk or syrup.

Ma's Dumplings Were Family Favorite

MY PARENTS *had seven mouths to feed during the 1930s. Times were hard for sharecroppers in the South, but our garden—and Ma's dumplings—got us through.*

Ma always made her dumplings with milk, butter, salt and pepper, rolling the dough thin, cutting it in tiny strips and dropping it in the pot to boil.

She made her dumplings with blackberries, apples and peaches. We canned lots of berries, so we'd be able to have berry dumplings all winter. Ma's chicken dumplings were delicious, too!

If there was ever a time when we didn't have anything to make for dessert, Ma made vinegar dumplings. They were delicious but took lots of sugar which was always hard to come by during those years.

Some days I still get a craving for Ma's dumplings, so I just take out a little pot and make a batch...but somehow, they're just not as good as hers. —Frances Caldwell, Spartanburg, South Carolina

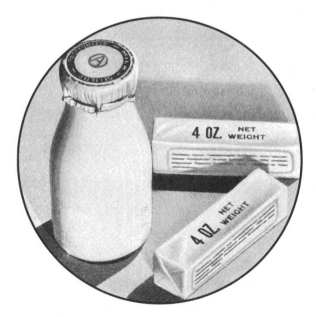

Hamburger Biscuits

Shared by Evelyn Williams-Hall, Sioux City, Iowa

2 cups flour
4 teaspoons baking powder
1/2 teaspoon salt
1/2 cup milk
1/2 cup lard
1 egg
1 cup hamburger

Mix a small amount of flour into hamburger. Crumble up until fine. Add flour, baking powder and salt. Then add lard, egg and milk and mix until touch is firm yet soft. Roll out and cut with a biscuit cutter. Then bake. The egg and hamburger gave the biscuits a different flavor, especially at a time when meat was so short.

'Mile-High' Baking Powder Biscuits

Shared by Merle Alexander, Hoquiam, Washington

2 cups flour
1/2 teaspoon salt
1/2 teaspoon cream of tartar
2 teaspoons baking powder
1/2 teaspoon baking soda
1 tablespoon sugar
1/2 cup shortening
2/3 cup buttermilk

Combine flour with salt, baking powder, cream of tartar and sugar in a bowl. Cut in shortening with two knives or pastry blender until the mixture looks like coarse meal. Add baking soda to buttermilk and pour into flour mixture. Stir until the dough forms a ball around a fork. Turn out onto floured board and knead. Pat into a circle 1/2 inch thick. Cut biscuits with 2-inch biscuit cutter. Place on ungreased baking sheet and bake at 450° for 15 minutes. **Yield: 16** biscuits.

Chapter 4

This and That

Cornmeal Mush, Fried Macaroni and Dandelion Gravy were some of the unusual dishes that became mealtime mainstays.

Preston County Buckwheat Cakes

Shared by Hazel Wiles, Smithfield, Pennsylvania

I WAS born and raised on a farm in Preston County, Virginia. During the Depression, nearly every family who lived there subsisted on Buckwheat Cakes.

Every fall my dad would take a wagonload of grain to the mill. The buckwheat was ground to make several sacks of flour to last the winter.

As the weather began to cool, we'd mix up a batch of batter and let it rise overnight. The next morning it was ready to make.

We always saved a couple cups of the batter as a starter for the next breakfast and from that time on we had Buckwheat Cakes each morning until the weather got warm again. Sometimes we had them for supper...and Mother served them to company at lunch.

In 1938, the famous Preston County Buckwheat Festival began and thousands of people attend it today. All the churches and restaurants serve Buckwheat Cakes and whole hog sausage.

  1 **quart water, lukewarm**
1/4 **large cake yeast** *or* 1
      package dry yeast
Buckwheat flour
1/2 **teaspoon baking soda**
  1 **teaspoon salt**
  1 **teaspoon white sugar**
  1 **teaspoon brown sugar**
1/2 **teaspoon baking powder**
  1 **cup warm water**
1/4 **cup buttermilk**
  2 **tablespoons milk**

In a gallon-size bowl, mix lukewarm water, yeast and enough buckwheat flour to make a stiff batter. Cover and let rise overnight. Next morning, take out 1 cup or so of batter for starter the next time and put it in the refrigerator. Dissolve baking soda, salt, sugars and baking powder in warm water. Stir in buttermilk and milk. Add to batter. Mix in more warm water to make batter thin enough to bake. Bake on a hot well-greased griddle. Lightly brown the griddle cakes. Now all you need to do is top them off with sausage, butter and maple syrup. To renew starter batter at night (or at least 3 to 4 hours before use), add 1 pint water to the cup or so of reserved batter and enough buckwheat flour to thicken. Next morning do the same as before. After several mornings, you may need to add about 1/4 teaspoon more yeast to the starter.

Grandma's Scrapple

Shared by Stanley Shifferd, Hendersonville, North Carolina

1-1/2 cups yellow cornmeal
5-1/2 cups cold water, **divided**
1-1/2 teaspoons salt
    1 pound pork sausage
Flour

In a large bowl, mix cornmeal, 1-1/2 cups water and salt. In a pan, bring 4 cups of water to a boil. Add cornmeal mix to the boiling water and stir carefully until mixture thickens. Cook pork sausage in a frying pan. Stir into cornmeal. Pour mixture into 2 bread pans and cool thoroughly in refrigerator. When ready to serve, cut into 1/2-inch-thick slices. Flour lightly, then warm and brown in frying pan. Serve as is or top with syrup. Can be frozen until ready to serve.

Eggy Lasses

Shared by Iva Shaw, Moundville, Missouri

Molasses
Eggs, beaten

Heat molasses, stirring constantly. Stir in beaten eggs and cook until eggs are done. Pour over pancakes, biscuits or hot bread.

Homemade Noodles

Shared by Virginia Elliott, Naples, Florida

1 cup plus 1 heaping
   tablespoon flour
2 tablespoons milk
1 egg plus 1 yolk
1/2 teaspoon salt
Broth

On a bread board or in a large bowl, make a mound of the flour with a hollow in the middle. Beat milk, eggs and salt together with a fork. Place in the hollow. Mix together from the outside in toward the middle until you have a rather stiff dough. Let sit for a couple of minutes and then roll out in two batches, as thin as you can get it. Keep flouring the dough as needed and roll up tightly. Slice the rolled dough into thin strips. Separate at once and hang over a broomstick or spread out on a table or counter to dry at least 2 hours. Ten minutes before serving, drop into gently boiling broth, stirring constantly so that the noodles do not stick together. The noodles will be ready to serve when no longer doughy— only your taste will tell for sure. The clinging flour will have thickened the broth and you will have a rich soup.

Comforts

Shared by Mrs. Kenneth Hess, Midland, Michigan

2 eggs
1 cup sugar
1/2 teaspoon salt
3 cups flour
1 cup sweet milk
1 teaspoon baking powder
Lard

Beat eggs and sugar together. Add remaining ingredients. Have a deep pan of hot lard ready and drop in a spoonful of the mixture at a time. When these are baked on one side, they should be turned over.

Four-Generation Dressing

Shared by Gail Hollingsworth, Tuscaloosa, Alabama

1 cup cornmeal
3/4 cup buttermilk *or* milk
3 eggs, *divided*
1/4 cup oil
4 slices bread
2 cups chicken broth, *divided*
1/2 cup celery, chopped
1/2 cup onion, chopped
1/2 cup green pepper, chopped
1-1/2 teaspoons poultry
 seasoning
1/8 teaspoon black pepper

In mixing bowl, combine cornmeal, buttermilk, 1 egg and oil. Bake at 450° for about 20 minutes. When corn bread is done, crumble with 4 slices of loaf bread. Pour on 1 cup of chicken broth and add celery, onion, green pepper, poultry seasoning, black pepper, 2 eggs and remaining cup of chicken broth. Mix well and bake at 450° for 1 hour.

When Food Ran Low, Grandma Came to the Rescue

MY HUSBAND CAME *from a very large family and one of our favorite places to go was Grandma's house for Sunday dinner.*

It wasn't unusual to have two or three tables of hungry folks to feed, so my cousins and I helped Grandma in the kitchen.

One Sunday, we ran out of food before it was our turn to eat. I'll never forget how Grandma told us not to worry and that she'd whip something up in a jiffy.

She took some shelled corn cobs and put them on her wood stove with a little bit of water and set them to boil while we finished cleaning up the kitchen. Then she made some homemade buttermilk pancakes with soda and egg.

We had the best homemade syrup from those corn cobs—just as sweet as honey. I'll always remember that special Sunday—and that special Grandma. —Delores Hedrick, Coalton, West Virginia

Candied Cranberries

Shared by Billie Blanton, Kingsport, Tennessee

3/4 cup white sugar, *divided*
1/2 cup water
1/2 cup fresh whole cranberries

Line small cookie sheet with waxed paper. In a heavy-duty medium saucepan, bring 1/2 cup sugar and water to a boil. Stir until sugar dissolves. Continue boiling for about 6 minutes until mixture reaches 238° on candy thermometer (soft-ball stage). Remove from heat and stir in cranberries. Let stand 3 minutes until berries are tender but retain shape. Using a slotted spoon, carefully transfer cranberries to prepared cookie sheet. Let stand until almost dry, about 20 minutes. Place remaining sugar on plate and roll cranberries in sugar until completely coated. Store cranberries in sugar. **Yield:** 1/2 cup.

Nut Hash

Shared by Claudine Howard, Coal Valley, Illinois

2 tablespoons bacon
**   drippings**
2 tablespoons onion, chopped
1 cup green pepper,
**   chopped**
1 cup celery, chopped
1 cup milk
2 tablespoons peanut butter
1 cup peanuts, chopped
1 quart cooked potatoes,
**   chopped**
Salt and pepper

Saute onion, green pepper and celery in drippings until tender, not brown. Add milk, peanut butter, peanuts, cooked potatoes and salt and pepper to taste.

Unusual Sandwich Was a Depression-Era Favorite

I GREW UP on a farm in South Dakota during the Depression and one of my favorite foods was a little unusual.

I would take a piece of toast, rub a piece of raw garlic over it, then spread it with goose fat and sprinkle it with salt. It doesn't sound good now, but we loved it back then! —Ethel Jass, Roseville, Minnesota

Lemon Crackers

Shared by Rosalie Trigg, Millersport, Ohio

2 eggs
2-1/2 cups sugar
1 cup butter
2 cups milk
1 tablespoon (1/2 ounce or 3 drams) lemon oil
4 tablespoons (2 ounces) baking ammonia
Flour

Mix eggs, sugar and butter and beat until very light and fluffy. Add milk, lemon oil and baking ammonia. Blend in enough flour to make a soft dough. Roll out about 1/4 inch thick. Cut diamond-shaped pieces the size you like. Prick with a fork. Bake about 12 minutes at 450°. Watch to make sure they don't burn and be careful when opening oven door. The ammonia will be strong. The longer they stand, the more like a cracker they will get.

Cinnamon Pancakes

Shared by Hilda Evans, Richwood, Ohio

1-1/4 cups flour
  1 cup buttermilk *or* sour milk
  1 egg
1/2 teaspoon baking soda
  1 tablespoon melted butter
  1 teaspoon baking powder
Cinnamon and sugar mixture
Bacon grease

Combine all ingredients except cinnamon-sugar mixture. Mix well. Pour batter into a hot skillet and fry in bacon grease. Brown on one side, then flip and brown on other side. Break pancake into small pieces while browning. Sprinkle with cinnamon-sugar mixture and serve.

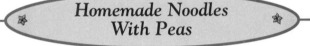

Homemade Noodles With Peas

Shared by Peggy Willits, North Palm Beach, Florida

  2 eggs
1-1/2 tablespoons cold water
  2 teaspoons salt, *divided*
1-1/2 cups flour, sifted
1/2 cup butter
  1 1-pound can early peas, drained

Beat eggs, water and 1/2 teaspoon salt until eggs are thickened and lemon-colored. Stir in flour. Add more flour if necessary to make a stiff dough. Knead lightly to work flour in. Divide dough in half. Roll dough out on lightly floured surface until it is very thin. It should be about 12 inches square. Place the dough between dish towels to partially dry. Repeat with other half of dough. Roll up each portion of dough in a jelly-roll fashion while it is still soft enough to do so. Cut into 1/2-inch-wide strips and spread out between towels to dry thoroughly before cooking. Melt butter in a small saucepan. Add peas and keep warm over low heat. Cook noodles in 6 cups rapidly boiling water with 1-1/2 teaspoons salt. Boil uncovered, stirring occasionally until just tender— about 10 minutes. Drain in colander and combine with peas.

Depression-Style Mush

Shared by Jesse Sholes, Williamsport, Pennsylvania

POP'S JOB at the foundry wasn't steady, and when the Depression hit, he had no job at all. He took work as a jack-of-all-trades in a hotel. It meant long hours and low pay.

I was the ninth of 10 children and Mom had to do the best she could with very little money. We had chicken or hamburger once a week—our Sunday dinner was a real treat.

Cornmeal Mush was one of our weekly staples. Mom served it at breakfast with a pinch of sugar and a little milk. We often ate mush fried in lard and spread with homemade jelly for lunch or dinner. It wasn't our favorite meal, but it was a good way for Mom to stretch what little food she had and keep us all fed.

2 **pounds cornmeal**
2 **gallons fresh water from pitcher pump**
1 **tablespoon salt**
Milk
Sugar
Lard

Put all ingredients in a large pot. Mix well and boil until it looks like mush. For breakfast, add a dash of milk and a pinch of sugar. For lunch or dinner, grease 5 or 6 bread pans with lard and fill with remaining mush to top. Allow to set until firm. Turn pans over onto a large plate. Cut into 1/2-inch slices. In heavy frying pan, fry slices of mush in lard until browned on both sides. Serve hot with homemade jelly or chowchow.

93

Beans and Corn Bread Were Simple, Filling Fare

AS THE YOUNGEST of three children, I learned firsthand how to feed a family during the Depression.

My father worked 6 days a week as a track maintenance man for the railroad, so we children did the cooking.

Many of our suppers included corn bread, navy beans and potatoes. Before bedtime, we'd put the beans in a pot to soak. The next morning, we'd drain them and add bacon rind, salt and onion if we had it. Then the kettle went on the wood stove to boil and we'd head off to school three blocks away.

We'd come home at noon, add water to the beans and make a lunch of tea and peanut butter sandwiches. We'd have preferred milk to tea, but getting cold milk was a chore!

Our only means of refrigeration was the fruit cellar. To keep our milk cold, we sealed it in quart jars and lowered it on short chains into the water cistern.

There was never enough time at lunch to remove the cistern lid and very slowly and carefully draw up a jar of milk. If we pulled the chain too quickly, the jar would swing against the cistern wall and break.

After school, it was time to build a fire in the kitchen range, make corn bread and cook the potatoes. That would be our supper along with the beans, molasses and a glass of cold goat's milk. We ate very well for the times— nothing fancy, but plenty of it.

—Alice Pixler, Whiting, Iowa

Tomato Gravy

Shared by Ruth Miller, Shreve, Ohio

1 quart tomato juice
1 cup water
Pinch baking soda
1 teaspoon salt
1/2 cup brown sugar
1/2 cup flour
3/4 cup milk

Heat tomato juice and water until almost boiling. Add baking soda, salt and sugar. Thicken with flour and milk and bring to a boil, stirring constantly. Serve over fried potatoes with a slice of buttered bread.

Egg Pie

Shared by Mary Hix, High Point, North Carolina

2 pie crusts, 8 or 9 inch
Eggs, boiled and sliced
Salt and pepper
Butter
Flour
Water

Place eggs on an 8- or 9-inch pie crust. Add salt and pepper, butter, a little flour and water. Put on top crust with a little flour and plenty of butter and bake.

Fried Macaroni

Shared by Opal Syndram, Roanoke, Indiana

1 pound elbow macaroni
3 to 4 cups water
1/2 teaspoon salt
Oil *or* margarine

Cook macaroni in water and salt until tender. Drain. In a large skillet, heat oil or margarine and fry macaroni until golden brown.

Grapenuts

Shared by Mollie Brant, Knob Noster, Missouri

3-1/2 cups wheat *or* graham flour
1 cup buttermilk
1 cup dark syrup
1 teaspoon baking soda
1 teaspoon salt

Line a cookie sheet with waxed paper. Mix ingredients and bake in 350° oven. Remove paper while cakes are hot. Cool. Break into small pieces and put in oven to dry completely. Cool and grind coarsely.

Marshmallow Sandwiches Were Childhood Treat

SUGAR AND FLOUR *were in short supply when we were growing up in the 1930s. So, we often satisfied our sweet tooth with marshmallow sandwiches made with soda crackers.*

We'd line a large pan with crackers, top each one with a marshmallow and put the pan in the oven.

Immediately after we took them out, we topped each marshmallow with another cracker. Those sandwiches were a special tasty treat!
—Viola Hancock, Osborne, Kansas

Sea Foam Candy

Shared by Cynthia Becker, Pueblo, Colorado

3 cups light brown sugar
2/3 cup water
1 egg white, beaten

Boil sugar and water until it forms threads from spoon. Pour over beaten egg white and beat until it begins to set. Drop by teaspoonfuls onto plate or waxed paper.

Shared by Mrs. Albert Stutzman, Goshen, Indiana

Handful dandelion greens
2 tablespoons butter
2 tablespoons lard
1/3 cup flour
1/2 cup water
2 cups milk
Salt and pepper
1 teaspoon vinegar
2 eggs, boiled and sliced

Soak dandelion greens for 1/2 hour in hot salted water. Drain. Melt butter and lard in a black skillet. Add flour and stir with spatula until nice and brown. Stir in 1/2 cup water. Add milk slowly, mixing until smooth. Add vinegar and dandelion greens. Salt and pepper to taste. Mix in eggs. We served this over mashed potatoes.

Popcorn Was Frequent Sunday Supper

I WAS A CHILD during the Depression and spent a lot of time at my grandparents' farm while my mother ran a restaurant in a small town nearby. There was no electricity at the farm and water was pumped from the well.

Since Granny and Grandpa had a garden, cows and chickens, there was never a lack of food. Grocery shopping wasn't like it is nowadays. We'd buy mostly staples like flour, laundry soap and if there was a little extra money, maybe a small bag of chocolate drops.

For Sunday suppers we often had popcorn and milk. We'd put the popcorn in a bowl, pour milk over it and eat it like cereal. Then the kerosene lamps would be lit and we'd play either dominoes or Chinese checkers. —Sally Price, Rushsylvania, Ohio

Neighbor's Gift Saw Folks Through Hard Times

I GREW UP in central Florida during the 1930s. There were seven of us in the family—three boys and two girls—and our parents worked hard to put food on the table.

We had a neighbor who was a World War I veteran. Each Saturday morning he'd walk the 3 miles to town to pick up the commodities the government gave to veterans—cheese, syrup, canned meat, vegetables, milk, coffee, sugar, rice, beans and yellow grits.

The grits were, of course, ground corn. Our neighbor didn't like the taste. He asked my mother if she'd like to have them—she wasn't about to turn down food of any kind with five children in the house! That's how we came to have plenty of yellow grits every week.

I never developed a taste for them and went hungry many a time rather than ask, "What's there to eat?"

But those yellow grits—and our neighbor's generosity—unquestionably helped pull our family through those hard times.

—Robert Bronson, Eustis, Florida

❧ Switchel (Haymaker's Drink) ❧

Shared by Beulah Bowden, Orrington, Maine

1 gallon water
1 cup molasses
1-1/4 cups vinegar
2 cups sugar
1 teaspoon ginger

Mix all ingredients and serve.

Vinegar Taffy

Shared by Betty Florence, Taylorsville, Kentucky

1 cup sugar
2 cups dark corn syrup
2 tablespoons butter
1 tablespoon vinegar
1/4 teaspoon baking soda
1 teaspoon vanilla

Combine first 4 ingredients in saucepan. Bring to boil over medium heat. Stir constantly until sugar is dissolved. Continue cooking to hard-ball stage (a small amount dropped into cold water forms a hard ball). Remove from heat, stir in baking soda and vanilla. Beat mixture until smooth and creamy and pour into buttered pan. When cool enough to handle, pull with fingers until candy is satiny and light-colored. Pull into long strips and cut into desired lengths. Wrap pieces in wax paper.

Mom's Dressing

Shared by Jill Cooper, Riverdale, Georgia

1/4 cup vinegar
3 tablespoons sugar
1 tablespoon butter
3/4 cup water
1 tablespoon flour
1/2 teaspoon dry mustard
1/2 teaspoon salt
2 eggs, beaten

Bring vinegar, water and butter to a boil. Remove from heat and whisk in sugar, flour, mustard and salt. Whisk in 2 beaten eggs and mix well. This would be used like mayonnaise.

Egg Custard

Shared by Carolyn Kelly, Albemarle, North Carolina

MY AUNT'S house was the family gathering place when I was growing up during the Depression.

My favorite childhood memories are of the times we'd spend on her front porch, which was covered with beautiful wisteria vines.

We'd make popcorn balls and my aunt would have some of her cocoa fudge on hand. For entertainment, she'd gather the children around and play "Fox and Geese"—she made the board and pegs herself.

Whenever anyone was sick, my aunt would make another of her specialties, Egg Custard, to take to the person. The recipe had been passed down from her grandmother. Today I still try to carry on this tradition using that old family recipe.

2 **tablespoons cornstarch**	Combine sugar with 2 heaping tablespoons cornstarch. Add the remaining ingredients and mix well. Pour into a pie shell. Sprinkle with nutmeg. Dot with butter if desired. Bake at 350° until firm.
2/3 **cup sugar**	
3 **eggs, beaten**	
Dash salt	
1 **teaspoon vanilla**	
Nutmeg	
Butter	

100

Pepper Relish

Shared by Mrs. C. L. Sawyer, Moyock, North Carolina

1 dozen *each* green and red
    bell peppers
2 glasses water
14 onions, ground
2 cups sugar
2 tablespoons salt
2 tablespoons celery seed
Vinegar

Remove seeds from peppers. Grind peppers, then place them in water and let them come to a boil. Drain. Add ground onions, sugar, salt and celery seed. Cover with vinegar and boil until tender. I use this relish in my potato salad. It's also good served with meats and vegetables.

Kids Ate Well at 'Sauerkraut Bee'

I LIVED IN a small community in Michigan during the Depression. My parents owned an acre of land next to our home and we planted lots of vegetables and fruit to get us by.

Mother canned everything possible—peaches, pears, tart cherries, huckleberries, pickles—and we always had a big crock of sauerkraut in the root cellar.

In those days, making sauerkraut was a "bee" of sorts. Neighborhood women got together and brought cabbages, cutting boards, salt, crocks and a dish to pass.

We children played while our mothers toiled, cleaning and shredding the cabbage, layering it in crocks, salting each layer and repeating the process until a crock was full.

Then they'd place a heavy weight on top, drape a cloth over that, and the crock was ready to go into the root cellar and ferment.

We children ate a lot of that sweet-tasting raw cabbage as it was being shredded. I still like to eat raw cabbage today!

—Mrs. Kenneth Hess, Midland, Michigan

Shared by Karen Angle, South Mountain, Pennsylvania

1-1/2 heads cabbage
1/2 peck green tomatoes
1-1/2 pounds brown sugar
6 onions
12 green peppers
1/2 ounce whole cloves
1/2 ounce brown mustard
1/2 ounce mustard seed
1-1/2 ounces celery seed
1 teaspoon black pepper

Chop ingredients, add spices and stew for 2 to 3 hours. Pack hot into hot canning jars. Consult canning guide for processing times.

Ad Took Us From Rags to Riches

BACK IN 1934 it was so hot and dry in Iowa, the only vegetable we could grow on our farm was green beans.

We were thankful for what we had—but we did get tired of those beans! One day, my two brothers and I saw an ad in our hometown newspaper, The Coon Rapids Enterprise, offering to buy clean rags.

We had plenty of those! So, we gathered them up, went to town and made our big sale—for 15¢.

After we collected our earnings we had to decide what to spend it on—a big decision for three kids.

We loved canned pork and beans but decided to base our choice on how much we could get for our money. We finally chose dry beans and we asked our mother to bake them for us. They sure were good and a change of pace!   —Berneice Johnson, Duncanville, Texas

103

Irish Potato Candy

Shared by Nettie Gilstrap, Panama City, Florida

1 Irish potato, about egg size
1 pound confectioner's sugar
Peanut butter
Nuts, finely chopped
Red and green cherries, chopped

Peel, dice and boil potato until tender. Drain and mash. Add sugar a little at a time. Mixture will be soupy at first. Keep adding sugar until mixture can be rolled out. Roll out like a pie crust. Spread thin layer of peanut butter over top. Then sprinkle with chopped cherries and finely chopped nuts. Press down into peanut butter. Roll up jelly roll style. Slice and serve.

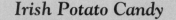

Pickled Eggs and Red Beets

Shared by B. Margaret Kinsey, Anthony, New Mexico

Beets
  1/4 cup brown sugar
  1/2 cup vinegar
  1/2 cup cold water
Small cinnamon stick
   3 to 4 cloves
   4 to 5 hard-boiled eggs,
      shell removed

Boil enough young beets (until tender) to fill a quart Mason jar. Skin and set aside. Mix brown sugar, vinegar, cold water, cinnamon and cloves. Add beets and boil together for 10 minutes. Let cool enough so you can comfortably handle the ingredients. Pour into a glass jar. Refrigerate beets in this liquid for several days. Remove the beets and store in another glass jar. Refrigerate. Add eggs to the vinegar mixture. Refrigerate eggs for another 2 days before using.

Brine for Meat

Shared by Dorothy Diesen, Rock Valley, Iowa

8 pounds coarse salt
3 pounds brown sugar
3 ounces saltpeter
6 gallons water

This amount is for 100 pounds of beef or pork. Heat water until it boils. Add salt and saltpeter. When it cools a little, mix all ingredients thoroughly. Let mixture get cold, then add meat. Leave bacon in brine for 10 days. Leave ham in for 5 weeks. Turn meat every week.

Sorghum Mill Made Sweet Memories

SOME OF MY *earliest memories are of helping Mom and Dad make sorghum molasses during the Depression years.*

Dad had one of the few sorghum mills for miles around and come fall, all the neighbors brought their sorghum cane to be made into molasses.

Dad and Mom, along with my brothers and sisters, would feed the fresh-cut cane into the mill to press out the juice.

A horse was hitched to a long pole and he'd walk around in circles powering the mill and pressing out the juice that would be boiled into molasses.

My job was to ride the horse. I felt mighty important doing that job—nobody told me the horse would have gone around in endless circles without a rider. In fact, I was grown up before my parents told me they put me on the horse to keep me out of the way!

We couldn't afford sugar, so Mom used sorghum molasses all year long to sweeten our oatmeal, glaze a ham, or bake gingerbread cookies. We learned to love sorghum as a sweetener in most everything.

—Leroy Orsburn, Wewoka, Oklahoma

Aunt Lois' Chili Sauce

Shared by Elaine Truitt, Palmetto, Florida

MY AUNT LOIS made wonderful Chili Sauce and I still have special memories of the way that aroma filled her kitchen.

I spent summers with her at Paw Paw Lake near Watervliet, Michigan and when her tomato crop was ripe, we'd can pints and pints of the delicious sauce.

Since Aunt Lois didn't like Chili Sauce, I was her taste-tester during the process—a job I loved.

During the cold Chicago winters, I'd remember all the fun Aunt Lois and I had when Mom would serve her Chili Sauce with our pot roast dinner—and that same aroma would fill the air at our house.

8 quarts tomatoes, peeled and quartered
1 red pepper, finely chopped
2 cups green pepper, finely chopped
3 cups onion, finely chopped
4 cups vinegar
2 tablespoons salt
2 cups sugar
3/4 teaspoon hot red pepper

Spice bag
3 tablespoons whole cloves
3 cinnamon sticks
2 tablespoons whole allspice
Or
1 tablespoon pickling spice
2 teaspoons cinnamon
1 teaspoon ginger

Measure tomatoes after peeling and quartering them. Place tomatoes in a 3-gallon container. Cook vigorously and stir occasionally until reduced to 1/2 the volume, about 2 hours. Add sweet red and green pepper, onion, vinegar and salt. Reduce heat and cook 45 minutes. Add sugar and spice bag. Continue cooking mixture slowly, stirring occasionally until sauce is thick, about 45 minutes. Remove spice bag and stir in hot red pepper. Pack sauce into hot sterilized pint jars leaving 1/2 inch at top. Consult a canning guide for processing directions. When I make this now, I update the sauce by freezing rather than hot packing.

Chapter 5.

Casseroles

Hamburger, noodles, potatoes
and other staples made filling
fare that helped stretch the
budget.

Lima Bean Casserole

Shared by Esther Weinreich, Esmond, Illinois

DURING the Depression, my mother had to bake seven loaves of bread three times a week to feed everyone at our table, which included eight children, plus my grandfather and the hired man who lived with us.

Mother often made Lima Bean Casserole to feed that hungry group. She always made this recipe with fresh cream from the farm.

Today, I'm the only one in the family who makes this casserole. My two children love it! These days I double the recipe so I can give my son and his family a dish. My brothers and sisters also ask me to make Lima Bean Casserole for family gatherings. It never fails to bring back pleasant memories.

1 pound dry baby lima beans
1 large *or* 2 medium onions, sliced
3/4 cup brown sugar
1/2 pound sliced bacon, cut in thirds
Salt and pepper
Milk

Soak and cook limas as directed on package. Drain. In a 2-1/2-quart casserole, layer as follows: one half of the lima beans, one half of the onion, one half of the brown sugar and one half of the bacon. Repeat layers, pouring milk over top until milk is visible. Bake at 350° for 2-1/2 to 3 hours. Cover if it browns too much. **Yield:** 6 to 8 servings.

Slumgullion

Shared by Karen Smigla, Hayward, Wisconsin

1 pound bacon, cut into 1-inch pieces
1-1/2 pounds elbow macaroni, cooked and drained
2 large onions, cut up small
1 large can tomatoes, with juice and cut in small pieces
Salt and pepper to taste

Brown bacon and onions well and drain off fat. Add cooked macaroni and tomatoes. Salt and pepper to taste and cook until tomatoes are heated through.

Lamb's-Quarter Egg Casserole

Shared by Florence Hershey, Seattle, Washington

4 tablespoons shortening
6 tablespoons flour
1-1/2 teaspoons salt
1/4 teaspoon pepper
3 cups milk
2 cups lamb's-quarter greens, cooked
4 hard-boiled eggs, sliced
1 cup cornflakes, crushed *or* dried bread crumbs

Melt shortening in saucepan. Add flour, salt and pepper and blend well. Blend in milk gradually, stirring constantly and continue cooking until thickened. Add lamb's-quarter and eggs and place in shortening-coated casserole. Cover with cornflakes or bread crumbs. Bake in 425° oven for 30 minutes. **Yield:** 6 servings.

Tame Rabbit Casserole

Shared by Anne-Marie LeBlanc, Memramcook, New Brunswick

Rabbit, cut in pieces
    1 tablespoon butter
    1 teaspoon olive oil
Salt and pepper
    1 clove garlic
Onions
    1 can tomato sauce
    3 bay leaves
Pinch oregano
Pinch parsley

Fry rabbit on all sides in butter and olive oil. Salt and pepper the pieces. Fry garlic and onions. Combine tomato sauce, bay leaves, oregano, parsley, salt and pepper. Pour over rabbit and cook slowly at 300° for 2 hours. Serve with noodles or rice.

Baked Eggs and Rice

Shared by Hilda Evans, Richwood, Ohio

    6 to 8 eggs
    2 tablespoons cream
Salt and pepper
    1 cup rice
    2 cups water
    2 to 3 cups tomato juice
Cornstarch *or* flour
Pinch sugar

Break eggs into buttered muffin tin (do not beat eggs). Add cream, then salt and pepper to taste. Bake eggs until firm in 350° oven. While waiting for the eggs to bake, cook rice in water until done. In a separate pan, heat tomato juice and add enough cornstarch or flour to thicken. Salt to taste and add a pinch of sugar. Place rice on a platter. Arrange baked eggs on rice and pour thickened tomato juice over the top.

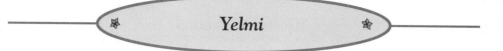
Shared by Roberta Holiday, Fort Worth, Texas

2 tablespoons bacon *or* ham
    drippings, *or* butter
Fresh green beans
Onion, sliced
Ripe tomatoes, sliced
Salt and pepper
Paprika
   1/4 cup water
Bits of leftover ham *or* lamb

Put drippings in a kettle. Add a thick layer of green beans, a layer of onion and a thick layer of tomatoes. Season with salt, pepper and generously with paprika. Pour in water and ham or lamb. Cover tightly and simmer for at least 1 hour.

Snap Bean and Hot Dog Dish
Still a Favorite Today

THERE WERE *nine children in our family, and though money was tight, my mother was a marvelous cook who made every meal delicious.*

We always raised a big garden and when the yellow snap beans were ready to eat, Mother made a wonderful dish. First she'd cut up about two quarts each of yellow snap beans and potatoes. Then she'd take hot dogs and slice them very thin. She'd cook everything together and add a big pat of butter.

She no doubt used only four or five hot dogs and made a meal to feed 11 people. It was one of our favorites.

I introduced this dish to my husband and now when yellow snap beans are in season, I have to make it once a week—he loves it!
    —*Eleanor Swanson, Farmington, Connecticut*

Elephant Potpie

Shared by Leona Willis, Milwaukee, Wisconsin

WHEN MY SISTER and I were in our early teens, our dad started teaching us to make simple dishes.

Elephant Potpie was the first thing he taught us how to cook. Dad made up the name for the recipe. Of course, elephant wasn't actually an ingredient—the name made preparing and serving the dish fun. To this day my brothers and sister and even our grandchildren still call this casserole by that name!

We'd serve it with homemade bread and butter, and often have chocolate cake with fresh whipped cream for dessert. During the Depression years we lived on a small farm where food was plentiful—what a blessing!

2 **pounds bulk pork sausage or wieners, cut into bite-size pieces**

2 **large cans sauerkraut, drained (bulk can be used)**

1 **large onion, chopped**

2 **teaspoons salt**

20 **to 25 medium to large potatoes**

Butter *or* oleo

Cook and whip potatoes, adding enough milk to make them fluffy. Add salt to taste. Line bottom of 9- x 12- x 2-inch cake pan with sausage. Bake at 350° until golden brown. Drain off excess grease. Cover meat with sauerkraut and onion. Spread potatoes over dish, hitting with back of spoon to form peaks. Dot with butter or oleo. Bake at 350° for 40 to 45 minutes or until peaks of the potatoes are golden brown and crispy.

112

Poor Man's Casserole

Shared by Carl Allman, Savannah, Missouri

1 small head cabbage
2 large potatoes
1 large onion, diced
1-1/2 pounds lean hamburger
1 teaspoon cumin
1/2 stick butter *or* margarine
Salt and pepper to taste
Dash paprika

Cut cabbage into cubes, salt and pepper to taste and cook until well-done. Drain. Peel and quarter potatoes. Salt and cook until well-done. Drain and mash with butter. Potatoes should be fairly dry. Place hamburger in large skillet with onion and cook until well-done. Drain off fat. Stir in cumin. Line the bottom of an 8-inch-round and 3-inch-deep baking dish with cabbage. Place meat mixture on top and cover with mashed potatoes. Sprinkle with paprika. Bake at 350° for 25 minutes. **Yield:** 4 large servings.

Hamburger Wiggle

Shared by Toni Beverly, Germantown, Tennessee

1/2 medium onion, chopped
1 tablespoon bacon drippings
or butter
1 to 1-1/4 pounds lean
ground beef
1 can niblet corn, with juice
1 can cream of mushroom soup
1 quart milk (more or less depending on your preference of soupy or thick)
4 to 5 medium potatoes, peeled and thinly sliced
Salt and pepper

Saute onion in bacon drippings. Add ground beef and brown. Stir in corn and soup. Add milk and potatoes. Heat but *do not boil* until potatoes are tender. This tastes better if made ahead of time and reheated. Skim off fat when cold.

Goulash

Shared by Esther Cochrane, Los Angeles, California

1/2 cup carrots, diced
1/2 cup potatoes, diced
1 cup water
1/2 cup peas
1/2 cup small red beans
1/2 pound hamburger *or* ground round
1 8-ounce can tomato sauce

In a pan, combine carrots, potatoes and water. Simmer until barely soft. Add peas and red beans, simmering for 5 more minutes. In a frying pan, fry hamburger, drain off fat and add to above. Stir in tomato sauce and vary the liquids according to taste. Simmer about 20 minutes or more to blend flavors.

Shepherd's Pie

Shared by Terese Snyder, Marquette, Michigan

1 pound ground beef
2 cups potatoes, mashed
1 small onion, minced
1 egg yolk, well beaten
Salt and pepper
Garlic powder

Saute onion and meat for 10 to 15 minutes over medium heat until fat from meat is rendered and onion is limp. Stir occasionally. Drain and discard fat. Season and place meat in bottom of a pie plate. Top with mashed potatoes and smooth with a spatula. Brush potato with egg yolk. This will give the appearance of a pie when baked. Bake for 30 minutes at 350° or until pie is golden.

Buttered Noodles with Cracker Crumbs

Shared by Muriel Schneiter, Altamonte Springs, Florida

1/4 cup butter
1 package saltine crackers
1 package noodles

Melt butter in large frying pan. Roll out crackers until they are fine crumbs. Place crumbs in the melted butter and fry on low heat until crackers turn brown. Cook noodles. Drain and put in frying pan with the crumbs. Turn them over so that all noodles are coated with crumbs. Serve with a boiled potato.

Meat-and-Potatoes Dish Was Welcome Change

OUR DAILY MENU in the 1930s usually consisted of oatmeal for breakfast, cornmeal mush and milk at noon, and any kind of soup for supper—as long as it was meatless vegetable.

But once in a while my Pennsylvania Dutch grandmother celebrated. She'd grease a baking dish and spread a layer of mashed potatoes on the bottom. Next she'd add a layer of roast beef cut into small pieces, then top it off with more potatoes.

The casserole would go into the oven until it was hot and the top was well-browned. She served this dish with gravy.

Grandmother's "celebration" meals included dessert—baked apples. She cored them, poured a syrup made of brown sugar and water over the top and baked them. The stuffing was usually raisins with more brown sugar syrup.

Cooking was more art than science for Grandmother. She didn't bother measuring quantities. Each of her special meals required creativity since food was often scarce during the Depression.

—Donald Lang, Kane, Pennsylvania

Corn Pudding

Shared by Blanche Richards, Glendale, Arizona

1 1-pound can cream-style corn
1/4 cup butter
2 eggs, beaten
1/2 teaspoon salt
1/3 cup cracker crumbs
1/4 cup onion, finely chopped
1/4 cup green pepper, very finely chopped
2 tablespoons pimiento, chopped

Mix all ingredients together. Bake in 1-quart casserole at 350° for 45 minutes.

Grandma's Casserole

Shared by Virginia Hill, Visalia, California

1 cup onion, chopped
1 green pepper, cut in strips
2 tablespoons margarine
1-1/2 pounds lean ground beef
1 teaspoon salt
1/2 teaspoon black pepper
1 tablespoon sugar
1 quart tomatoes
1 15-ounce can tomato sauce
2 cups water
1 8-ounce package wide noodles, uncooked
1 8-ounce package mozzarella cheese, sliced

In a Dutch oven, saute onion and green pepper in margarine for 3 minutes. Add ground beef. Brown meat, breaking up with a spoon. Stir in salt, black pepper, sugar, tomatoes, tomato sauce and water. Heat mixture for 15 minutes. In a 13- x 9- x 2-inch glass baking dish, layer tomato/beef mixture and noodles. Top with cheese. Make sure noodles are well covered by sauce. Cover with foil and bake at 350° for 45 minutes. Cut and serve as you would lasagna. **Yield:** 8 to 10 servings.

116

Noodle Bake

Shared by Elsa Watters, Lakewood, Ohio

ONE of my favorite memories from childhood is of coming home cold from an afternoon of playing in the snow and finding the warm kitchen filled with the aroma of my favorite dinner cooking.

I'd put my wet mittens on the shelf below the stove and wait impatiently for that delicious German meal to be served.

Along with her German Beef Roast and Sweet-Sour Cabbage, Mother always served a family favorite—Noodle Bake.

It tasted extra-good because my mother and grandmother made their noodles from scratch. I still serve this casserole today, but I take the easy way out. Even with store-bought noodles, this dish never fails to remind me of the warmth of home!

2 tablespoons onions, chopped
2 tablespoons green pepper, chopped
1 tablespoon margarine
3 cups noodles, cooked and drained
1/4 cup margarine, melted
3 eggs, separated

Simmer onions and peppers in the 1 tablespoon of margarine. Fold this along with 1/4 cup melted margarine into noodles. Beat egg yolks well. Add to above mixture and refrigerate. The next day or when ready to bake, beat the egg whites stiffly and fold in. Pour into greased casserole. Place casserole in pan of hot water and bake at 350° for 20 minutes or until knife comes out clean.

Hot Dog Casserole

Shared by Helen Styczen, Lisle, Illinois

1 large green pepper, cut into long slivers
1 large onion, cut in half, then into long slivers
1 clove garlic, chopped
2 tablespoons butter *or* bacon fat
4 medium potatoes, peeled and cut into 2-inch pieces
6 to 8 hot dogs cut into 1/2-inch pieces
8 ounces tomato sauce
1/2 cup water
Dash cinnamon
Salt and pepper
1/2 teaspoon brown sugar

Preheat oven to 350°. In a large frying pan, place green pepper, onion and garlic in butter. Saute until slightly tender but not soft. Set the pan aside. Place potatoes in a large saucepan filled with salted water. Cook the potatoes at a slow boil for 10 minutes. Drain and set aside. To prepare sauce, put tomato sauce, water, brown sugar and cinnamon in a large bowl. Add salt and pepper to taste. Mix well. Add the sauteed vegetables, potatoes and hot dogs to the sauce. Mix well. Place the mixture in a greased 2-quart casserole dish. Cover the dish and bake for about 45 to 50 minutes. Allow the dish to set for a few minutes before serving. **Yield:** 6 servings.

Shipwreck

Shared by Merle Egeland, Stockton, California

MY FAVORITE MEAL during the "Dirty '30s" was a dish my grandmother and mother made called Shipwreck.

They made it in a big casserole pan and there was usually enough for two or three meals.

Today, the simple ingredients—potatoes, ground beef, rice and kidney beans—wouldn't be considered all that special. But during tough times it was a meal fit for a king!

I still love this casserole—it was one of the best dishes we had as children.

4 potatoes, sliced
2 large onions, sliced
1 pound ground beef
1 cup rice, cooked
1 15-1/2-ounce can kidney beans
1 10-3/4-ounce can tomato soup

Using a 4-quart casserole dish, layer the ingredients as follows: potatoes, onions, ground beef, rice and kidney beans. Continue layering until all ingredients are used. Pour tomato soup over all and bake at 325° for about 1-1/2 hours or until the potatoes are done.

Meatless Loaf

Shared by Claudine Howard, Coal Valley, Illinois

1 cup rice, cooked
1 cup peanuts, crushed
1 cup cottage cheese
1 egg
1 tablespoon oil
1 teaspoon salt

Combine all ingredients. Bake in a loaf pan in 350° oven for 30 minutes or until loaf is set.

Shared by Coralyn Lawrence, New Hartford, New York

1 can corned beef
6 potatoes (in skins)
1 medium onion
1 large can evaporated milk
1 can whole milk
1 stick margarine *or* butter
Salt and pepper

Boil potatoes (do not overcook) and then chill. Grind corned beef with firm, peeled potatoes. Grind onion (add more onion if desired). Melt butter and add to meat, potatoes and onions. Mix well and add the milk. Add salt and black pepper to taste. Pour into a greased casserole, dot with butter and strips of green pepper. Bake at 350° for 1 hour or until it forms a nice brown crust.

Mom's Ingenuity Made Mealtime Special

FOR ME, *the mid-1930s are filled with wonderful childhood memories despite the Great Depression.*

My father was out of regular work for 3 years and was employed by the WPA. My mother made and sold baked goods to help provide for my sister, brother and me. We never went hungry—everyone worked together and I'm sure that was the secret.

One of our frequent dinners was Meat Pie, though it had very little meat in it. It was simply potato pie with leftover meat from a previous meal. Mother would add chopped celery, onions and carrots if she had them.

This dish was usually served with warm milk, but if we were really lucky, there might be gravy from the meat to water down, heat and serve over it.

Mothers during those days were good at making the simplest meals tasty, attractive and nutritious.

—*Mrs. William Atwell, Zieglerville, Pennsylvania*

Ham Casserole

Shared by Clara Ehrke, Bradenton, Florida

2-2/3 cups egg noodles
3 cups milk
3 tablespoons butter
2 teaspoons salt
1/4 teaspoon pepper
4 tablespoons cheese, grated
1/2 cup green beans
1/2 cup asparagus
1/2 cup carrots, diced
2 cups ham, cubed

Cook noodles until done. Drain. Combine all ingredients. Bake in buttered casserole at 325° for 1-1/2 hours. Buttered crumbs may be used on top.

Cabbage Rolls

Shared by Vicky Giesbrecht, Saskatoon, Saskatchewan

1 large head cabbage
3/4 cup long grain rice, uncooked
2 cups ground pork
1 cup ground beef
1 medium onion
Salt and pepper

Remove cabbage heart, separate leaves and rinse in cold water. Mix together the rice, pork, beef, onion, salt and pepper. Place 1 tablespoon of the mixture on each leaf (or half leaf) and roll up. Tuck ends in last. Place in roaster or large casserole dish. Cover with water or tomato sauce. Cook about 1-1/2 hours at 325° to 350°. When cabbage is cooked, rice will be soft.

❊ Grandma's Mexican Casserole ❊

Shared by Kimie Taziri, Fort Collins, Colorado

MY PARENTS, who were originally from Japan, learned to appreciate the foods of many different cultures and passed this on to their children as we grew up in Wyoming.

A favorite Depression-era dish was Grandma's Mexican Casserole. Grandma used whatever meat she had available back then and fed a family of nine with it. One of the meats she commonly used was bologna—an economical lunch meat in the '30s.

Like most cooks of her day, Grandma didn't write many recipes down, so I had to rely on my memory and help from my family to duplicate it.

3 medium potatoes	1 15- to 16-ounce can
Flour	kidney *or* pinto beans,
2 eggs	optional
1 teaspoon water	Add herbs of choice *or*
5 tablespoons oil, *divided*	1 teaspoon cumin
1 large onion, chopped	1 tablespoon parsley
1/2 green pepper, chopped	1 to 2 tablespoons chili
1 or 2 cloves garlic, chopped	powder
1 rib celery, chopped with	1 teaspoon sugar
leaves, optional	1 tablespoon lemon juice
1 pound ground beef	Black pepper
1/2 pound ground pork	
1 15- to 16-ounce can	
tomatoes	
1 8-ounce can tomato sauce	
1 15- to 16-ounce can cut	
green beans	
1 15- to 16-ounce can	
whole corn	
1 15- to 16-ounce can	
creamed corn	

Boil potatoes until done but still a bit firm. Cool well. Slice thin. Dust with flour. Beat eggs with water until frothy. Preheat 3 tablespoons oil in large skillet to medium hot. Dip floured potato slices in egg mixture, drain slightly and carefully put into hot oil. Cook until golden brown. Remove to paper towels and drain. Set aside. In a large Dutch oven, heat 2 tablespoons of oil and saute the onion, green pepper, garlic and celery. Add ground beef and ground pork. Brown well and drain off excess fat. Add the tomatoes, tomato sauce, green beans, whole corn, creamed corn, kidney beans, cumin, parsley, chili powder, sugar, lemon juice and black pepper. Bring stew to a boil and cut heat to simmer. Carefully fold in prepared sliced potatoes. Continue simmering for approximately 30 minutes to blend all the flavors.

❀ Baked Macaroni and Cheese ❀

Shared by Angie Fiddler, Winchester, Virginia

        7 **cups water**
Dash salt, optional
      15 **ounces elbow macaroni,
          uncooked**
Margarine *or* butter
        2 **cups cheddar cheese,
          shredded**
        3 **cups mozzarella cheese,
          shredded**
      25 **saltine crackers**
2-3/4 **cups milk**

Boil water and salt over medium heat in large saucepan or Dutch oven. Add macaroni and stir. Reduce heat and simmer for 10 minutes or until macaroni is tender, stirring occasionally. Drain well. Grease bottom and sides of 13- x 9- x 2-inch baking pan with butter or margarine. Spread 1-1/2 cups macaroni in pan. Sprinkle 1 cup cheddar cheese over surface and top with 1-1/2 cups macaroni, spreading to sides of pan. Add 1-1/2 cups mozzarella cheese and top with another 1-1/2 cups macaroni. Follow this with 1 cup cheddar and 1 cup mozzarella cheese. Top with remaining macaroni and 1/2 cup mozzarella. Crumble saltines evenly over top, spreading to sides of pan. Slowly pour milk over crackers, flattening with fingers until macaroni is even and crackers are soggy. Bake at 350° for 45 minutes or until crackers are golden and cheese is melted. **Yield:** 12 servings.

Tomato Dish Was 'Simply' Delicious

I WAS BORN *during the Depression and our family managed to eat well even though some foods were scarce.*

I remember one dish well because it has become a treat in my family. It's called Baked Tomato and Bread.

We grew lots of tomatoes in our garden and when they were ripe, we peeled and stewed them for sauces and to "put up". But one batch was always withheld from the canning jars to use for this recipe. Mother would add whole kernel corn, salt and pepper and then tear up some day-old bread and put it on top.

She'd bake this casserole until the tomato juice bubbled up through the bread and it smelled wonderful. We'd eat it with a spoon when it was soupy and a fork when it got more done. My mother couldn't go wrong with that dish! It was a simple and satisfying recipe—getting fancy would have ruined it.

—Carolyn Shank, Virginia Beach, Virginia

❧ Egg Noodle Casserole ❧

Shared by Annette Markowski, Wakaw, Saskatchewan

4 cups egg noodles, cooked
4 eggs, well beaten
1-1/2 cups milk
1/4 cup butter, melted
1 cup raisins, washed
1/2 cup white sugar
1 teaspoon vanilla
1 teaspoon salt

1 teaspoon cinnamon, optional

Cook noodles, rinse with cold water and drain. Mix all ingredients with noodles. Pour into greased 9- x 13-inch pan. Cover loosely with foil. Bake at 350° until set, approximately 1 hour. Cut into squares.

Mom's Chicken Dish

Shared by Merle Swendsen, Brooksville, Florida

THOUGH I moved away several years ago, I spent most of my life in upstate New York and consider that part of the country my roots.

When I was growing up, my mom always said you could make a meal with whatever you had in the house—and that's just what she did. Her Chicken Dish always lured us to the table without having to be called.

I still have her handwritten book of good old recipes. My children cherish it and whenever they visit me in my new home, they read it from cover to cover.

2 tablespoons butter
1 pint whole tomatoes
2 small zucchini, thinly sliced
1 small eggplant, peeled and cubed
1 medium onion, sliced
1 medium green pepper, cut in pieces
1 small can mushrooms
2 teaspoons salt
1/2 teaspoon oregano
1/2 teaspoon basil
Dash pepper
2-1/2 cups cooked chicken, cubed

Melt butter in large skillet. Add vegetables and mix. Cover and simmer gently until tender and crisp, about 15 minutes. Add seasonings. Stir in chicken until thoroughly heated. Serve on toast squares or over rice.

Liver Casserole

Shared by Joyce Scott, Kirkland, Washington

WITH A FAMILY of nine sons and her husband to feed during the Depression years, my mother-in-law had to make maximum use of every scrap of food coming into the house.

Many times she had precious little to work with. When I married her son, she gave me the recipe for her Liver Casserole that she often made during those years. It's become one of our family's favorites too!

3 medium onions, chopped
1 to 2 tablespoons butter
2 to 3 cups liver, cut into bite-size pieces
2 eggs, hard-cooked and cut up

Sauce

2 tablespoons flour
2 tablespoons butter *or* bacon grease

Hot water

1 teaspoon paprika
1/2 teaspoon dried crushed sage *or* 1 teaspoon poultry seasoning (modern version)
1 tablespoon prepared mustard
2 to 3 tablespoons vinegar

In large pan, saute onions in butter. Add liver and brown. Add the hard-cooked eggs and set aside while preparing sauce. In saucepan, stir together flour, butter or bacon grease and enough hot water to make a thick gravy. Cook until thickened. Add paprika, sage or poultry seasoning, dried mustard and vinegar. Stir together. Add sauce to meat mixture and stir together. Place in 2- to 3-quart baking dish. Top with buttered bread crumbs. Bake at 350° for 40 to 45 minutes. More liver can be used if you have it left over from previous meal.

Corn Bread Dressing

Shared by A. Lee Hickman, Killen, Alabama

6 cups corn bread,
  crumbled
3 cups stale biscuits,
  crumbled
3 tablespoons fresh sage
1 teaspoon celery seed,
  optional
2 cups onion, chopped

3 eggs, beaten
1/4 teaspoon black pepper
Pork broth

Combine all ingredients and mix well. Place in a greased casserole dish and bake at 350° for 40 minutes or until nicely browned.

Noodle Dish Was a Weekly Favorite

FRIDAY SUPPERS *during the Depression years usually meant we'd be treated to one of my mother's special dishes.*

She would brown bread crumbs in butter, add pre-cooked noodles and top it off with a generous helping of applesauce. We always looked forward to this delicious treat.

It remains one of my favorite "comfort foods" today, but somehow it never tastes quite the same as it did when Mom made it. —Rita Ritter Fort Wayne, Indiana

Shared by Barb Anderson, Deer Park, Wisconsin

1/2 pound egg noodles
   (2 cups uncooked)
1-1/2 pounds ground pork butt
2 small onions, chopped
1 1-pound can tomato soup
1-1/3 cups water
1/2 pound grated cheese
2 teaspoons salt
1/8 teaspoon pepper

Cook the noodles 20 minutes in boiling salted water. Drain. Cook meat and onions together until brown. Mix meat, onion and noodles together. Add the tomato soup, water, grated cheese, salt and pepper. Bake in casserole in moderately hot oven or place in sauce pan and let simmer on top of stove for 30 minutes.

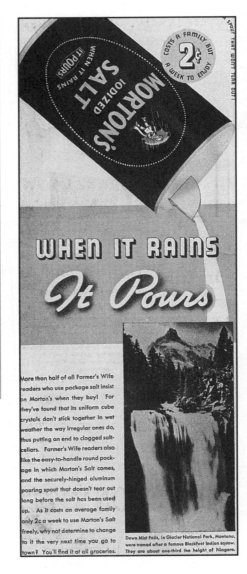

Mabel's Macaroni

Shared by Barbara Smith, Encinitas, California

I CAN REMEMBER *eating my mother's macaroni dish often in the 1930s. She made it whenever we had company and served it with a green salad and garlic bread.*

There were no set amounts to the recipe. She just used whatever was still in the cupboard.

She usually made it when we got together with three other families to play cards. The girls would bring a can of ripe olives and we'd eat them under the bed while we told ghost stories. We made our own fun during the Depression!

1/2 package large macaroni, boiled and salted	Croutons, crushed
1/2 pound bacon, cut into 1/2-inch pieces and fried	1/8 cup salsa, optional
1/4 cup onion, chopped and fried	Green peppers, optional
1 cup stewed tomatoes	Mix all ingredients (except croutons) well. Put into a large casserole dish. Top with croutons. Bake at 350° for 35 minutes.
1/2 cup tilamook cheese, grated	

Baked Hominy

Shared by Myreda Jeffras, Annapolis, Maryland

2 tablespoons onion, chopped	2 cans yellow hominy, drained
2 eggs, beaten	
Pepper	Saute onion. Mix all ingredients well and pour into a baking dish. Bake in a 350° oven for 25 minutes.
1 tablespoon margarine	
1 cup cream	

Creamed Beans Have Old-Fashioned Flavor

MY MOM *was able to make three meals out of the huge pots of beans she would cook.*

On the first day we would have bean soup and hot homemade biscuits. The next day would bring baked beans and on the third day she would cream the last of that lot.

She would mix the bean juice with equal parts of fresh cream and sorghum molasses, season it with salt and pepper, then pour it over the beans and bake it for an hour.

I've changed the recipe today and use condensed milk and brown sugar. But either way, the taste is great!

—Doris Hicks, Lyman, Wyoming

Mom's Scalloped Tomatoes

Shared by Marlene Barnes, Hardesty, Oklahoma

3 cups onions, sliced
4 tablespoons butter, melted
2 tablespoons flour
1 teaspoon salt
Dash cayenne pepper
Dash black pepper
1 2-1/2-pound can tomatoes

1/2 cup cheese, grated *or*
    buttered bread crumbs

Saute onion in butter. Add next four ingredients together with tomatoes. Sprinkle cheese or crumbs on top and bake.

Cheese Noodles

Shared by Marlene Kouba, Regent, North Dakota

1/2 package noodles *or*
    macaroni
2 cups dry cottage cheese
2 cups cream
3 eggs
Raisins, optional
Sugar to taste
Cinnamon

Boil noodles or macaroni according to directions. Drain. In a bowl, mix cottage cheese, cream, eggs and sugar. Butter a cake pan or casserole. Put noodles in pan, pour creamed cheese mixture and raisins over noodles. Sprinkle with cinnamon. Bake at 350° for 30 minutes.

Preparing a Meal for a Family Of 11 in the 1930s

EARLY in the morning we would go to the garden and pick a large bucket of green beans. We'd also pull onions and pick cucumbers, beets and cabbage.

Then we'd head to the potato patch and dig potatoes with a kitchen fork, making sure to get the biggest potatoes at the top of the soil.

When we got back to the house, we'd snap the green beans and cook them in a large heavy kettle for 3 or 4 hours. Next we'd wash and cook the beets. When they were tender, we would peel and slice them, then cover them with sugar, vinegar and salt.

The next step was to put on a large kettle of water to boil and head for the chicken house. There we would pick two or three young roosters (we kept the pullets for our eggs) and get them ready to cook.

Next we'd make a trip to the apple tree for apples to fry or bake and after putting them on to cook, it would be time to put the chickens on to fry. While the chicken was frying, we would put sugar, vinegar and salt on the cucumbers and onions we'd cleaned earlier in the day.

After that we'd chop the cabbage to make slaw, add potatoes to the green beans and make two or three large pans of biscuits or corn bread in the old wood stove. By that time, the chicken would be done and it would be time to make the gravy and put dressing on the cabbage.

Finally, the preparations were finished and the meal would be ready for serving. Everyone had to be seated at the table before we could begin eating. There was a long black bench on one side of the table and chairs on the three other sides.

If we had company that day, some people would have to wait to eat. But we never filled our plates and went someplace else to eat. Everyone ate together at the table.

—Ruth Jackson, Mount Vernon, Illinois

Chapter 6.

Meat

Dishes

Meat was an infrequent item on tables of
the day and cooks concocted clever ways to
get the most for their money.

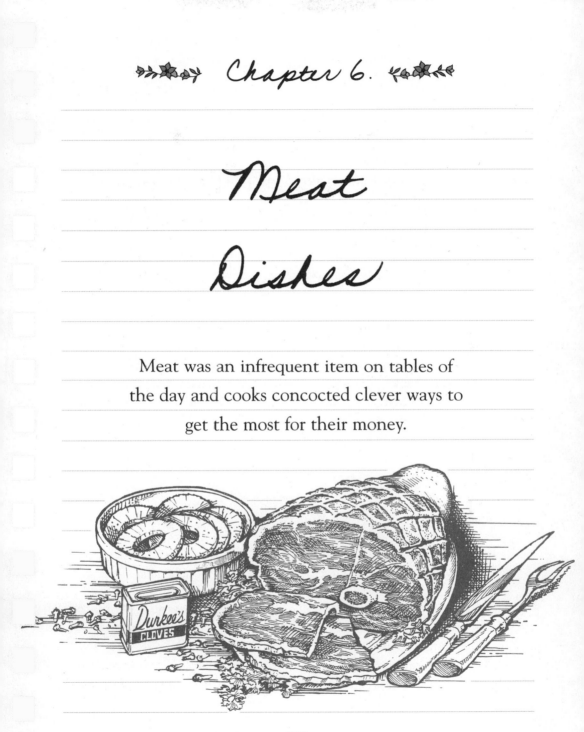

Poor Man's Stew

Shared by Dianna Larosee, Cumberland, Rhode Island

WHEN I was growing up, our family struggled to make ends meet, usually "borrowing from Peter to pay Paul".

As a result, my mother learned how to make very tasty dishes using only a few ingredients. Even though we didn't have much to spare, there was always enough to eat at our house.

One of my mother's specialties during the Depression was Poor Man's Stew. The recipe was handed down from my grandmother.

Cloves are the secret ingredient and my mouth still waters when I think of that tasty combination of meat and spices!

5 to 6 cups water
2 large onions, thinly sliced
2 pounds hamburger
10 medium potatoes, sliced
1/4 inch thick
Salt and pepper to taste
5 to 6 whole cloves

Combine water, onions, salt and pepper and boil until onions are clear. Crumble pieces of hamburger into mixture and bring to a boil. Add cloves and potatoes. Cover and simmer for 15 minutes. Water will reduce to 1/2 of recipe.

Hobo Stew

Shared by Margaret Porter, Conneaut Lake, Pennsylvania

1 large can tomatoes
1 medium onion, chopped
1 tablespoon sugar
1 large can baked beans
1 large ring bologna, cut into
1-1/2-inch slices

In a large pan, combine tomatoes and onion. Cook until onion is soft. Add sugar and beans. Mix well. Add bologna. Cover and cook mixture slowly until meat is done. Season to taste.

Beef Potpie

Shared by Mrs. Otto Baker, Decatur, Indiana

THIS Beef Potpie recipe is a favorite from my Depression-era childhood. Back then, our family enjoyed it with many different kinds of meat.

My grandfather hunted and fished to put food on the table and trapped for furs to earn extra money.

When I first tasted this dish it was made from squirrel stock. When squirrel was out of season, we'd make the potpie with beef.

1 can beef
3 cans water
2 potatoes, diced
1 teaspoon salt
1 tablespoon parsley
Dash pepper

Cook together until potatoes are done. Meanwhile, make potpie dough.

Potpie Dough
  2 cups flour

3 tablespoons lard
1/2 teaspoon salt
Water

Blend flour, lard and salt evenly. Add enough water to form a pie dough. Roll dough out into a thin circle. Cut into 2-inch squares. Drop into boiling broth mixture. Stir well. Reduce heat. Cook about 20 minutes. This potpie can be made ahead of time. The longer it steeps, the better the flavor will be.

Canned Steak

Shared by June Formanek, Belle Plaine, Iowa

1 cup salt
1 cup white sugar *or* 2 cups
  brown sugar
1 gallon rainwater
Pork *or* beef steak

Bring salt, sugar and water to a boil. Let stand overnight. Put 1 cup of the brine in a 1-quart jar. Fill with meat (pork is the best). Cold pack for 1 hour.

Poor Man's Steak

Shared by Viola Trittipo, Albion, Indiana

1-1/2 pounds ground beef
1/2 cup fine crackers *or* bread crumbs
1/2 cup water
2 teaspoons salt
1/2 teaspoon pepper
Flour
1 can mushroom *or* celery soup

Mix first 5 ingredients together. Pat mixture out in flat pan to 3/4 inch thick. Refrigerate overnight. Cut into serving-size pieces. Roll pieces in flour and brown in small amount of fat. Lay pieces in baking pan. Cover with soup. Bake in preheated 300° oven for 1-1/2 hours. **Yield:** 4 to 6 servings.

Fresh Pork Boil

Shared by A. Lee Hickman, Killen, Alabama

Fresh pork backbones, ribs, liver and heart
Water
Salt and pepper

Combine desired amount of fresh pork and cover with water. Bring to a boil. Skim off residue as it forms or boil a few minutes, then pour off all water and residue and add new water. Add salt and pepper. Cook until well-done. Dip off enough broth to make Corn Bread Dressing, leaving plenty of broth to cover meat.

Corn Bread Dressing
6 cups corn bread, crumbled
3 cups stale biscuits, crumbled
3 tablespoons fresh sage
1 teaspoon celery seed, optional
2 cups onions, chopped
3 eggs, beaten
1/4 teaspoon black pepper

Combine all ingredients. Add pork broth and mix well. Place in greased casserole dish and bake at 350° for 40 minutes or until browned.

Depression Days Called for Special Etiquette

MEAT of any kind was hard to come by during the Depression, but Granny had a special way to get around that.

She'd often tie a clean cotton string around a piece of salt pork and hang it in some cooking pinto beans to give the dish a meaty flavor.

Before the beans were completely done, she'd remove the salt pork and save it for another meal.

One time a neighbor borrowed her salt pork and when she didn't bring it back for a while, Granny asked her where it was. Turns out they'd eaten it! You can bet Granny never lent them any meat after that breach of etiquette.   —Jean Baker, Weatherford, Texas

Pepper Pot Hash

Shared by L. D. Wilson, Canal Winchester, Ohio

     4 to 5 slices bacon
  1/4 cup onion, chopped
     3 cups potatoes, diced
     1 teaspoon salt
  3/4 teaspoon pepper
Water

Brown bacon, potatoes and onion in a skillet. Add salt and pepper. Add water until barely covered, then bring to a boil. Let simmer for an hour. Do not let it boil dry, but cook down until juice is somewhat thick. Serve with cold canned tomatoes or stewed tomatoes and creamed sweet rice for dessert. This is good made with leftover beef roast and can be stretched into an extra meal.

Mama's Oven-Fried Chicken

Shared by Merle Alexander, Hoquiam, Washington

MAMA'S Oven-Fried Chicken was the envy of all who knew her. Every Sunday it turned out the same—tender and juicy on the inside and crispy, but never greasy, on the outside. Her "secret" has always stayed in the family and I make this dish the same way today.

Along with Mama's chicken, Sunday dinners featured corn on the cob, "zippy" green beans, thick slices of vine-ripened tomatoes, cucumbers and onions in vinegar, mashed potatoes and creamy chicken gravy.

Mama's other specialties were her "mile-high" baking powder biscuits and wild blackberry pie. We enjoyed freshly churned butter, clear amber honey in the comb for our biscuits and delicious homemade ice cream alongside homemade pie.

The menu doesn't really sound like a meal for hard times—especially for a family of 12—but that's exactly what it was. We raised everything ourselves, except for the blackberries which grew wild in the meadows and were picked by children too young to get jobs.

During the Depression, "a chicken in every pot" was the slogan of hope. Those Sunday dinners made our hearts beat with hope. We had a chicken in our pot and we knew we'd get by.

I still get a warm feeling when I make this meal and remember those days.

2 2-1/2-pound frying chickens
Sweet skim milk
2 cups dry bread crumbs, rolled fine
2 teaspoons salt
2 teaspoons paprika
1 teaspoon lemon pepper
1/2 teaspoon thyme
1/2 teaspoon tarragon
1/2 teaspoon parsley
1/2 teaspoon sage
1/3 cup cooking oil

Cut chickens into serving pieces. Place in a shallow baking pan and completely cover with milk. Let stand at least 1 hour. In a bowl, combine bread crumbs, salt, paprika, lemon pepper, thyme, tarragon, parsley and sage. (1 tablespoon poultry seasoning can be substitut-

138

ed for herbs.) Make a well in the center and pour in cooking oil. Mix until oil is completely absorbed by the crumbs. Set aside. At cooking time, put coating mix in a paper bag. Take chicken out of milk bath a few pieces at a time. Shake off excess milk and drop in the bag of coating mix. Shake vigorously to coat evenly. Lay pieces of chicken in lightly oiled baking pan. Bake at 450° for 40 minutes or until juices run clear. Prepare Rich Creamy Gravy as directed in the following recipe.

Rich Creamy Gravy
    3 tablespoons drippings
    3 tablespoons flour
1-1/2 cups cream
Salt and pepper
Butter, optional

If necessary, add enough butter to make up the 3 tablespoons of drippings. Combine the drippings and flour in skillet and cook over low heat until lightly browned. Add cream very slowly, stirring constantly. Season to taste with salt and pepper. Cook for about 7 minutes.

P'or Soles

Shared by Sharon Aden, Dongola, Illinois

Pork backbones
    2 to 3 quarts water
    2 to 3 cups white cornmeal
    1/4 cup flour
Salt and pepper to taste

Boil pork backbones in water until tender. Remove backbones from pot. Combine cornmeal, flour, salt and pepper and enough of the pork broth to form walnut-size balls. Heat the remaining broth to boiling. Drop the balls of cornmeal mixture in the boiling broth and cook until firm.

Wash-Day Boiled Dinner

Shared by Patricia Spiegle, Grove, Oklahoma

2-1/2 to 3 pounds ground
 sausage
 12 to 14 small potatoes,
 peeled (if new garden
 potatoes are used, scrub
 skins off)
 6 to 7 large carrots, scraped
 and cut in half lengthwise
 1 medium-large head
 cabbage, washed, cored
 and quartered
1-1/2 tablespoons salt
 2 to 3 teaspoons pepper

Put a large kettle 2/3 full of water on range to boil. Shape sausages into balls (just a little larger than a golf ball). When water comes to a full boil, drop sausage balls, potatoes, carrots and cabbage into the kettle and add the salt and pepper. Let ingredients boil about 3 to 4 minutes, then turn heat down to a simmer and put a loose lid on the kettle. Let simmer for at least 2 hours. **Yield:** 12 to 13 servings.

Depression Fish

Shared by Mildred Hutchison, Mt. Vernon, Illinois

3 cups flake hominy
 2 cans mackerel
Cornmeal
Oil *or* lard

Cook hominy and let it cool. Mix in the mackerel. Spread mixture into a 15- x 9- x 3-inch pan and refrigerate until solid. Cut in squares or strips and roll in cornmeal. Fry in oil until brown. Turn fish one time while frying.

City Chickens

Shared by Beverly Carman, Broadway, New Jersey

DURING the Depression, fried chicken was the main course at Sunday dinner for many families. But at our house, the entree we loved most of all was City Chickens.

Though they were a substitute for the real thing, we all loved the taste and we kids even helped make them.

The younger kids saved their popsicle sticks all summer and the older kids helped crush the cornflakes and even mold ground veal and pork into drumstick shapes around the sticks.

After the shaping was done, Mother would fry the "drumsticks" until they were golden brown—just like fried chicken. Those City Chickens were fun to eat and fun to make!

1 **pound ground veal**
1 **pound ground pork**
4 **tablespoons water, *divided***
Salt and pepper to taste
2 **eggs**
2 **cups cornflakes**
2 **cans chicken broth**
Popsicle sticks

With a fork, mix together the veal, pork, 2 tablespoons of water, salt and pepper. In a bowl, beat the eggs and 2 tablespoons of water. Set aside. Place cornflakes in a large plastic bag. Roll with rolling pin, making small crumbs. Take a popsicle stick and shape meat mix over 3/4 of the stick to form a "drumstick". Roll in egg mixture, then in crumbs. Fry 2 or 3 at a time until golden brown, turning often so all sides are browned lightly. Use oil as needed. Lay on paper towel and drain after frying. Place 8 or 10 "drumsticks" in 9- x 13-inch baking dish. Pour chicken broth over all. Cover with foil and bake for 2 hours at 325°. Uncover and bake 25 minutes more.

Crock Did Double Duty as Family Freezer

BECAUSE *they didn't have refrigerators, many Depression-era cooks had to find creative ways to store food for later use.*

When my dad would butcher a hog, Mom would fry the pork chops until they were well-done. Then she'd get out her 6-gallon crock and put a layer of pork chops in the bottom.

Next she'd pour drippings from the frying on top and then make another layer. She kept it up until the crock was full. Then she'd put a cover on and keep it in a cold spot on the back porch.

On pork chop night, all Mom had to do was heat up the meat and make gravy with the drippings.

—Lois Lyman, Hampton, Iowa

Bologna Gravy

Shared by Annette Oppegard, St. Paul, Minnesota

2 tablespoons butter
2 tablespoons flour
2 cups milk
1 ring bologna, skinned and diced
1 can whole kernel corn, drained
Salt and pepper

Melt butter in skillet. Add flour and blend. Pour in milk, stirring constantly until mixture boils. Simmer until thickened. Add bologna and continue to simmer a few minutes. Salt and pepper to taste. Finally, add corn. Serve over mashed or boiled potatoes.

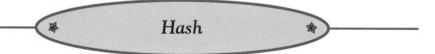

Hash

Shared by Barbara Iams Griffith, Helena, Montana

DURING THE DEPRESSION, *I don't ever remember a roast served to us as it is today—huge and done exactly as you like it with generous second helpings for the asking. I do know we had pot roast occasionally because of the end result…we got served Hash the next day.*

The first day, our roast slices were carefully carved before serving. The fact that Mama placed the portion on our plate told us that one slice was all we were going to get. It was no use asking for seconds.

Roast was served with mashed potatoes and gravy and homemade bread and butter. We could have all the potatoes and gravy we wanted until we emptied the bowl. The house rule was that anything we took on our plates, we finished—period. As a result we all learned to watch just how much we took.

Since there was only so much to go around, we traded freely. On Hash day, I always gave up my share and ate leftover gravy on bread.

In later, better years, my mother often made Hash. Daddy loved it more than roast. At that time she had a dependable gas stove and a much better frying pan, but she still got out the same grinder—over 50 years old—attached it to a chair seat, put a flat pan underneath it and fed in the leftover roast pieces.

Leftover roast *or* steak pieces
    1 small onion
Boiled potatoes
Salt and pepper
Leftover gravy *or* stock *or* water
    2 tablespoons bacon
        drippings *or* butter the
        size of an egg

Using coarse blade, grind meat and onion, or chop finely. Dice twice as many potatoes as you have in meat-onion mixture. Mix together and season with salt and pepper. Add just enough gravy so mixture hangs together. Bring a heavy pan with bacon drippings to sizzling. Press hash down firmly into pan in an even slab. Brown well, picking up pan and shaking it back and forth to loosen hash. When bottom is browned, use a spatula to turn hash over in as large a chunk as you can. Brown second side well. Just before serving, mix hash so browned portions are distributed evenly.

Twice-Cooked Chicken With Vegetables

Shared by Virginia Elliott, Naples, Florida

WHILE I was growing up, I lived with my grandparents in the small town of Bloomville, Ohio.

During the Depression, Grandma taught me a valuable lesson about getting the most out of food. She never made less than two meals from anything she put in a pot.

One of Gram's Sunday dinner specialties was Twice-Cooked Chicken with Vegetables. Before church, we'd pick the meanest old hen or rooster in the barnyard to be the main course.

While we were gone, it would simmer on the back of the stove. Even the feet were cooked, along with four or five onions from the cellar and a generous pinch of celery salt. We used that because fresh celery was rare.

When we got home, Grandma would send me back down to the cellar for a pan of potatoes, carrots, parsnips, turnips and more onions. While I scrubbed and peeled the vegetables, Grandma rolled out her noodle dough on the old tiger oak dining room table.

Once Gram cut the noodles into long yellow strips, I'd lay them out to dry on a broomstick that was propped between two chair backs. When she wasn't looking, I'd snitch one or two to eat raw!

By this time, the chicken would be tender and Gram would lift the pieces out and dredge them in flour and seasonings. The big black iron skillet smoked with hot home-drawn lard and while the chicken pieces gently browned, the vegetables I had cleaned would be boiled in the chicken broth.

I'd set the table while Gram mixed up a pan of biscuits, measuring the ingredients with her fist and fingers. Somehow, her timing was always perfect—crispy chicken, tender vegetables and crusty biscuits were all ready to be served at the same time. What a lunch!

For supper, we'd have Gram's homemade noodles she'd cooked in a pot of reserved chicken broth, already seasoned with the vegetables from our big dinner.

Dessert at both meals was any leftover biscuits broken up and topped with peaches and cream.

The memories of the time we spent preparing and enjoying those delicious Sunday meals will always be special to me!

1 stewing hen
4 medium onions,
   quartered
2 stalks celery, diced *or* 1
   tablespoon celery salt
1 tablespoon pepper
Water
Whole carrots, potatoes, turnips,
  parsnips and onions
Vegetable oil
2 tablespoons margarine

Coating
1 cup flour, sifted
2 tablespoons cornstarch
1 tablespoon salt
1 tablespoon pepper
1/2 teaspoon nutmeg

Combine chicken, quartered onions, celery and pepper in a large stewing pot with enough water to cover. Set to boil. Skim fat as necessary and reduce heat to simmer. Cover and cook 2 hours or until chicken is tender but not falling off bones. Remove chicken and add whole vegetables to broth. Use enough vegetables so each person has at least one of each kind. Combine ingredients for coating in a bowl. When chicken pieces are cool enough to handle, dredge in the coating. Gently fry until crisp, turning as needed, in 1 inch of vegetable oil to which 2 tablespoons of margarine has been added.

Ham Was the Secret to Mom's Lucky Dinner

MY MOTHER *was very good at making a little food go a long way and one of her favorite suppers for us children was a dish called Luck Hominy.*

    Mother would put on a pot of grits that had been ground from the corn we'd grown and then go to the smokehouse for a slice of country-cured ham.

    After the grits had simmered for a while, she cooked the ham, cut it into small pieces and stirred it into the grits before serving.

    It was called Luck Hominy because we were lucky if we got more than one small piece of ham!

    —*Mary Elizabeth Evans, Cameron, South Carolina*

Sausage and Cabbage Pie

Shared by Caroline Welch, Williamsport, Pennsylvania

MY DAD handed down to me many recipes he used during the Depression. After Mother passed away, he did all the cooking for my three brothers and me.

Dad came from a long line of chefs and he cooked in the lumber camps when he was 16 years old.

Every morning Dad made sure our breakfast was on the stove before he left for work. We ate homemade bread, oatmeal and sometimes fried potatoes with eggs mixed in. We never heard of cold cereal!

Our main meal was supper. We only had meat on Sundays and once a month or so, Dad would make his Sausage and Cabbage Pie. He'd trade a chicken or some eggs for a pound of sausage from a local hog farmer. Sunday dinners were always wonderful since Dad had the day off.

I don't know how he managed to do everything and take such good care of us. I only remember him sleeping 4 or 5 hours a night. I felt honored to have the wonderful father I did.

1 pound bulk sausage
1 small onion, chopped coarsely
1 small cabbage, cored and chopped
1 16-ounce can stewed tomatoes
1/2 teaspoon sugar
1/2 teaspoon salt
1/4 teaspoon pepper
1/4 teaspoon basil
2 tablespoons flour
1/4 cup water
5 large potatoes
1/4 cup milk
1 teaspoon butter
1/2 cup cheddar cheese, shredded

Brown sausage and onion in large skillet. Drain off grease. Add cabbage and cook uncovered for 15 minutes. Stir in tomatoes and seasonings. Then mix water and flour together and add to cabbage, stirring until thickened. Pour mixture into a 2-quart casserole dish. Meanwhile, boil potatoes, then mash. Add milk, butter and cheddar cheese to the potatoes and whip. Spread on top of cabbage mixture. Bake at 350° for 30 minutes.

Aromas of Home Leave Lasting Memories

DURING the Depression, Ma would buy the biggest piece of meat she could afford—usually a seven-bone or chuck roast—to feed Pa, Sis and me.

She'd put the roast in her blue porcelain roaster or an old cast-iron Dutch oven. Then it would go onto the giant "combination" stove. The stove used wood or coal on one end for heating the kitchen and cooking and had gas burners at the other end for summer cooking.

We grew a small garden in the backyard that provided us with vegetables and fragrant lilacs to brighten the table.

After the roast had cooked for a while, Ma added the potatoes and carrots we grew, along with some cabbage and onions that we'd swapped for.

After dinner, any leftover meat was cut up, put into the icebox on the back porch and saved for "Tuesday Stew". When that was history, anything that was left went back into the icebox for Vegetable Beef Soup later in the week.

To this day I can still remember the smell of those delicious meals at home. I've come close, but I can't duplicate them—even the lilacs.

—James Smit, Tustin, California

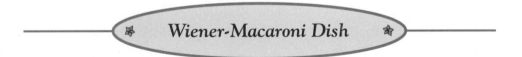

Wiener-Macaroni Dish

Shared by Bonnie Pinkerton, Wilsall, Montana

Wieners, cut into 1/4-inch slices
Onions, chopped
   1 can stewed tomatoes
Macaroni, cooked

Saute wieners with onions. Pour in the tomatoes and cook a few minutes. Add the macaroni. This can be made in any amount.

Salt Pork Gravy and Fried Green Tomatoes

Shared by Melody Wassell, Silvis, Illinois

6 to 7 slices salt pork
Green tomatoes
Flour
Salt and pepper
Milk
Water

Fry the salt pork slices and set them aside in a warm place. Slice tomatoes 1/2 inch thick. Season flour with salt and pepper. Dip tomato slices in flour mixture. Fry tomato slices in the grease from the salt pork until browned on both sides. Remove tomatoes to a plate and place in a warm oven. Pour all but 2 tablespoons of grease out of the pan. Thicken the grease with flour. Add a little milk and water and boil the mixture into gravy. Top the fried tomatoes with the salt pork and pour the gravy on top.

Hamburger Cups

Shared by Barbara Everitt, Waynesboro, Virginia

1-1/2 pounds ground meat
Salt and pepper
Onion, sliced
   3 tablespoons butter
   3 tablespoons flour
   2 cups canned tomatoes
   1 teaspoon sugar
Buttered bread crumbs

Grease deep muffin pans and line with meat. Press evenly over the bottom and up the sides. Place a slice of onion in each cup. Melt butter and stir in flour. When well blended, add tomatoes and cook until thick and clear. Add sugar, and salt and pepper to taste. Fill cups with mixture and place another slice of onion over the top. Sprinkle with buttered bread crumbs. Bake in 350° oven for about 35 minutes. Serve with a parsley garnish.

Flíéky (Confetti)

Shared by Georgiana Vacek, Western Springs, Illinois

MY MOST VIVID memories of the Depression are of the ingenious ways my mother used every morsel of food.

She saved bacon, chicken, duck and goose grease in separate jars and used it to add flavor to bland foods. She slowly simmered the skin from poultry until it resembled crisp bacon, then crumbled it and added it to biscuits or sprinkled it on top of meatless casseroles.

Mother also had a special way of carving chicken, adding a small portion of breast meat to each wing so it appeared that the bird had four drumsticks.

One of my mother's recipes which stretched scarce ingredients yet made for a filling meal was called Flíéky. Translated, the name means confetti. She used homemade noodles which brought down the cost, and she varied the amount of meat depending on what was left over.

As children we always knew that if Mother served split pea soup, the main course would probably be Flíéky, but we always enjoyed it.

1 medium onion, chopped
1/4 cup bacon grease *or* butter *or* margarine
1 pound broad noodles, boiled and drained
2 cups ham, finely diced
3 eggs, beaten
1 cup milk

Saute onion in bacon grease. Combine noodles, onion and ham. Put in buttered 3-quart casserole dish. Mix together the beaten eggs and milk. Pour over top. Bake at 350° for 45 minutes or until top is crispy. This was normally served with cold, boiled beets or cold, pickled beets.

Pork Cake

Shared by Lillian Marcotte, Woodstock, Vermont

2 cups molasses
1 cup sugar
1 cup salt pork, freshened, chopped
1 cup currants
1 cup raisins
1 tablespoon nutmeg
1 tablespoon cloves
1 tablespoon cinnamon

2 cups sour milk
2 teaspoons baking soda
Flour

Combine ingredients, adding enough flour to make a stiff batter. I don't have exact baking directions, but I think this was sometimes steamed for 3 hours.

Nature's Freezer Kept Meat Fresh Each Winter

I LIVED in the southeastern part of Colorado during the early '30s. If there was a Depression, we were unaware of it since money was scarce in the best of times and our way of life didn't depend on that commodity.

The first hard freeze meant it was time to butcher a cow. Mother would can part of it for the following summer and wrap the rest in a sheet. It would then be taken to the top of the windmill platform.

When the supply in the kitchen got low, Dad would cut off a big chunk of the frozen meat and the rest would stay frozen until we needed it.

Hogs were butchered in the fall also. The bacon and ham would be cured, pork chops cut and put down in a big crock with sausage. Melted lard would be poured over the meat to keep it fresh for future use. Mother also canned chicken for our winter food supply.

If we were poor, our dining table didn't show it. The "good old days" may be gone, but today the memories are still as clear as ever.

—Ella Dixson, Tillamook, Oregon

Shared by Corinne Brown, Gibson City, Illinois

I WAS a little girl during the Depression when Franklin D. Roosevelt was elected president.

There were five of us kids living on the farm in Michigan and we all had healthy appetites. So Mother became an expert at stretching a little meat into a satisfying meal.

One recipe she often used was called President's Dinner—supposedly a favorite of FDR. After nearly 50 years of marriage, my husband and I still enjoy this dish and our grandchildren think it's great.

I still have my mother's card with the recipe written on it. The card is getting dark and the ink is fading, but it holds a special place in my recipe box.

Wake up APPETITE

ONE OF THE 57

HEINZ TOMATO KETCHUP

6 medium potatoes, diced
6 carrots, sliced
2 medium onions, chopped
1 can peas
1 can tomato soup
1-1/2 pounds pork, partially cooked and cut into cubes

Mix all ingredients together and bake for 1-1/4 hours or until vegetables are tender.

American Chop Suey

Shared by Genevieve Purple, Murfreesboro, Tennessee

2 tablespoons butter *or*
  margarine
1 medium onion, chopped
1 green pepper, chopped
2 pounds hamburger
Salt and pepper
1 quart stewed tomatoes
1 package macaroni, cooked

In a large frying pan combine butter, onion, pepper and hamburger. Stir and chop up hamburger until well cooked. Add salt and pepper to taste. Stir in stewed tomatoes. In a saucepan, combine the hamburger mixture with the macaroni and let simmer for 15 to 20 minutes.

Grandma's Stuffed Roll

Shared by Margaret Pache, Mesa, Arizona

1 egg, beaten
1/2 cup quick-cooking oats
1 pound hamburger
Salt and pepper to taste
1/4 cup onion, chopped
1/4 cup celery, chopped
1/4 cup butter
1/2 teaspoon sage
Bread crumbs
2 tablespoons lemon juice
1 pound spinach, cooked
  and drained
4 eggs, hard-boiled and
  sliced
2 slices bacon

Mix egg, oats, hamburger, salt and pepper. Pat mixture into a 9- x 12-inch pan on waxed paper. In a saucepan, cook onion and celery in butter until tender. Stir in sage. Toss with bread crumbs and lemon juice. Spread over top of meat. Add spinach and hard-boiled eggs. Roll up meat like a jelly roll starting from narrow end. Press edge to seal ends. Transfer roll seam side down to a greased baking dish. Halve bacon strips crosswise on top of roll. Bake uncovered at 325° for 50 to 60 minutes. **Yield:** 6 to 8 servings.

Mom's Swiss Steak

Shared by Renee Riorden, Eagle Bay, New York

2 round steaks, 1 inch thick,
    (1 pound or more each)
Flour
    3 tablespoons cooking oil
    1 large onion, chopped
Salt and pepper
Leaves from 1 bunch celery,
    rinsed and cut from stems
1-1/2 cups homemade chili
    sauce
Boiling water

Place steaks (one at a time) on waxed paper and generously cover with flour. Pound the flour into steak. Turn steak over and repeat process. Steaks should now be about 1/2 inch thick. With sharp knife, cut each steak into 4 or 5 pieces. Heat cooking oil in Dutch oven. Saute onion. Remove and set aside. Brown steak pieces on both sides in single layer in the hot oil. Season to taste with salt and pepper. Remove and repeat for all steak pieces. Return all pieces to pan. Sprinkle with sauteed onions. Spread celery leaves over all. Pour chili sauce over all. Add enough boiling water to come up to the top of the steaks. Cover. Increase heat and when steaming, turn to low and simmer for 1-1/2 hours or until tender. Turn steaks once during cooking. **Yield:** 4 to 6 servings.

Salted Cod's No Money-Saver Now

WHEN WE children of the Depression talk about the meals of that time, common foods always come up.

One favorite I recall is salted cod. It came in a box for 10 or 15 cents. My mother would soak it to remove the brine, cream it and serve it over potatoes.

A few months ago, some friends and I were talking about it and I got the urge to buy a box of that salted cod. That old-fashioned penny pincher now costs between $7 and $8 a box—talk about sticker shock!

—Lillian Scieszka, Lansing, Michigan

Fried Chicken

Shared by Leona Mielke, Almena, Wisconsin

1/3 to 1/2 cup flour
1-1/2 teaspoons salt
1/2 teaspoon pepper
2 eggs, lightly beaten
1 cup oil *or* shortening
2-1/2 to 3 pounds frying
  chicken, cut into pieces

In a paper or plastic bag, combine the first 3 ingredients. Next, dip the pieces of chicken in the eggs. Put the chicken in the bag, a few pieces at a time, and shake in the flour mixture. Heat the oil in a large skillet. Add the chicken and brown over medium heat. When browned on both sides, remove the chicken and place in a roaster. Bake at 350° for 45 to 60 minutes until done. **Yield:** 4 to 6 servings.

Spanish Pot Roast

Shared by Nancy Schlinger, Middleport, New York

1 4-pound round-bone pot
  roast
1 tablespoon vegetable oil
2 tablespoons butter
1 large onion, chopped
2/3 cup Spanish olives, sliced
2 to 3 tablespoons olive
  juice
2 cups canned tomatoes
Salt and pepper to taste
1/4 cup flour
1/2 cup water

Brown pot roast in oil and butter in a Dutch oven until deep brown. Add onion, olives and olive juice. Crush tomatoes and pour over top. Add salt and pepper. Bring to a boil. Cover and simmer slowly for 2 to 3 hours until meat is tender. Remove meat and keep warm. Leave vegetables in pot and make gravy by adding 1/4 cup flour stirred into 1/2 cup water. Stir into juices and cook until thickened. Serve meat with gravy over top.

Pasty

Shared by Mrs. James Rodemeyer, Tucson, Arizona

Crust
1-1/2 cups vegetable shortening
1/2 cup boiling water
2 tablespoons milk
4 cups flour
1 teaspoon salt

Filling
1 pound pork, cubed
1 pound beef, cubed
4 medium potatoes, cubed
1 small rutabaga, cubed
1 medium onion, chopped
Salt and pepper to taste

Mix all crust ingredients together. On a floured surface, roll 1/4 of the crust out into a 10-inch circle. Mix filling ingredients together and place 1/4 of the mixture on one side of the circle. Fold over the other half and crimp edge as you would the top crust of a pie. Place on ungreased baking sheet and brush the top with beaten egg. Do not slit the crust. Repeat 3 times with remaining crust and filling ingredients. Bake at 350° for about 1 hour or until golden brown. **Yield:** 4 pasties.

Mulligan Stew

Shared by Jean Luehr, Racine, Wisconsin

2 pounds beef *or* hamburger, browned
1-1/2 pounds pork sausage, browned
1 16-ounce can lima beans
1 16-ounce can red kidney beans
1 16-ounce can peas
1 large bunch celery, diced
2 cups carrots, diced
3 cups potatoes, diced
2 large onions, diced
2 quarts tomatoes, crushed
Salt and pepper to taste

Mix all ingredients and bake for 2-1/2 hours at 300°.

Country Met City in Our Backyard

WE LIVED IN a small town in Missouri during the Depression. At that time there were no restrictions against having farm animals within city limits.

Even though we lived in a residential area, we had a cow, calf and pig being fattened for butchering. We also had a large pen of frying chickens and a chicken-yard full of laying hens.

My dad and mother were both raised on farms and they used what they'd learned there throughout their lives.

Our problem wasn't having enough to eat but getting the things we couldn't raise ourselves—like coffee, sugar, flour and spices. Luckily, Dad had a job with the railroad which paid for most of our staples.

The Depression hit hard in big cities where people weren't able to provide for themselves. We were some of the lucky ones.

—Phyllis Jordan, Marion, Ohio

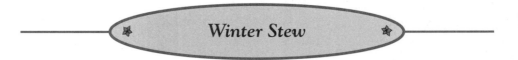

Winter Stew

Shared by Laurlie Morris, Akron, Ohio

1 pound stew beef, cut into chunks
2 onions, cut into chunks
4 carrots, cut into 1-inch pieces
1 15-ounce can tomatoes, chopped
1 large dill pickle, quartered, cut into 1-inch pieces
Salt and pepper to taste
1 cup sour cream
8 ounces broad noodles, cooked
Oil

In a heavy saucepan, brown beef on all sides in a little oil. Add onions, carrots, pickle, salt and pepper. Add tomatoes, liquid and all. Simmer until beef is tender. Add sour cream. Serve over hot noodles. **Yield:** 4 to 6 servings.

Loin of Pork Roast

Shared by Julia Kapinos, Norwich, Connecticut

6 to 8 pounds pork
1-1/2 tablespoons flour, sifted
1 tablespoon salt
1/2 teaspoon sugar
1 teaspoon ground mustard
1/2 teaspoon ground parsley
    flakes
1 tablespoon white pepper
1 cup applesauce
1/4 cup brown sugar

Dash cinnamon and cloves

Combine flour, salt, sugar, mustard, parsley and pepper. Rub over meat thoroughly. Roast uncovered for 3 hours at 325°. Mix applesauce, brown sugar, cinnamon and cloves and spread over meat. Continue baking for 45 minutes more or until meat is tender.

Tight Budget Called for Stretching the Meat

MY HUSBAND graduated in the late 1930s and jobs were tough to find. He finally was able to land one and after we figured out our weekly budget, there wasn't much left over for food shopping.

To get the most for our money, I shopped at the two markets in our neighborhood to get the best price on staples, vegetables and meat. To stretch the meat I bought, I came up with a strict schedule.

I'd buy a round-bone pot roast and cut out the largest portion for our Saturday night dinner. We would have it roasted with onions and a pinch of garlic and I'd serve more of the same on Sunday.

Monday's supper would be hot beef sandwiches and gravy. Tuesday I'd serve stew made from the smaller portion of the roast. Wednesday it was meat pie made from the leftover pieces of roast and stew, with a biscuit crust.

On Friday, we'd have soup made from the round bone I'd cut out previously and all of the leftover vegetables from the week's dinners.

We enjoyed these meals and my husband always complimented me on being a good cook.　—Lucella Bowman, Yucca Valley, California

Baked Chicken with Bacon and Vegetables

Shared by Lucille Stejskal, Florence, Alabama

4 chicken breasts
4 chicken legs
4 chicken thighs
Salt and pepper
2 cups carrots, sliced
1 cup celery, chopped
1/2 cup onion, chopped
8 slices bacon, cut in 1-inch strips and fried crisp
2 tablespoons bacon drippings
2 chicken bouillon cubes
1/2 cup water

Line bottom of casserole with chicken pieces. Salt and pepper to taste. Add carrots, celery and onion. Place bacon pieces on top. Spoon bacon drippings over all. Dissolve bouillon cubes in water and pour over top. Bake at 350° for 1-1/2 hours or until chicken and vegetables are tender. If necessary, add more water during baking to keep chicken moist. Serve with oven-browned potatoes or buttered noodles.

Leftover-Roast-Stretching Recipe Was Family Favorite

MY MOTHER *had lots of ways to get the most out of cuts of meat.*

She'd buy a pot roast and serve it with mashed potatoes and gravy, home-canned green beans and homemade applesauce.

The next day she would grind the leftover meat in her hand grinder and mix it with leftover mashed potatoes, gravy and onions. Then she'd form the mixture into patties, dip them in egg and water and cover them with bread crumbs she'd made from stale bread.

Next, she'd fry the patties and spoon tomato soup over each one. This was a frequent main dish at supper time and it sure was good!

—Marie Vanco, Medina, Ohio

Chapter 7.

Desserts

Sugar shortages didn't stop housewives
from coming up with special
treats for the family.

Polish Crullers

Shared by Anne Kulick, Phillipsburg, New Jersey

DURING the Depression, my mother worked in New York as a housekeeper and nanny. She sent her monthly salary back to Dad in Oxford, New Jersey.

He'd lost his job there when the iron-ore mine closed but still had to make payments on the family car. Dad worked with the WPA and on weekends, he'd make much of the food we'd eat during the week ahead.

Every Saturday Dad would bake 8 or 10 loaves of bread and several batches of Polish Crullers. He made a big bread box to store all the baked goods and they never got stale or moldy!

I have vivid memories of the neighbor kids pressing their little noses against the screen door while Dad fried the crullers. When he finished, Dad would give the kids some of the tasty treats and they'd run off down the street.

I still correspond with two of my childhood friends and to this day we reminisce about how good the warm bread tasted and how delicious those crullers were!

4 cups flour
3 teaspoons baking powder
3 large eggs
2 tablespoons butter *or* margarine, melted
1 cup sugar
2/3 cup milk
1/2 teaspoon vanilla
Pinch salt
Shortening

Sift flour, baking powder and salt together. Set aside. Blend butter, sugar, vanilla and eggs. Beat thoroughly. Add the milk alternately with the sifted dry ingredients. Roll out on floured board into a ball. Divide the ball into 4 parts. Keeping remaining portions covered, roll 1 section on the floured board to pie-crust thickness. Cut into strips 1-1/2 inches wide. Cut each strip into 4-inch pieces and slit each piece in center. Pull one end through the slit, forming a bow-like design. Deep-fry in electric frying pan at 325° using shortening only (no oil). Fry until golden brown, turning crullers to fry each side. Drain crullers on paper towel and when cool, roll them in powdered sugar. **Yield:** 6 dozen.

Christmas Suet Pudding

Shared by Doris Doherty, Albany, Oregon

1 cup brown sugar
1 cup carrots, grated
1 cup apples, grated
1 cup chopped suet *or* margarine
1 cup raisins
1 cup currants *or* mixed fruit
1 teaspoon *each* baking soda, salt, cinnamon, nutmeg, allspice
1 cup chopped nuts
1-1/2 cups flour

Caramel Sauce
1-1/2 cups dark brown sugar
3/4 cup corn syrup

4 tablespoons butter

Mix first 4 ingredients together. Add remaining ingredients and mix well. Pour into an ungreased tin. A 1-pound coffee can works fine. Set in pan with 2 or more inches of water. Put pan on stove and steam for 1-1/2 hours. Mixture will be soft. Remove from water and set tin in 325° oven for about 15 minutes to dry out. Remove from oven and let set for a day or 2. For sauce, combine all ingredients. Boil to soft-ball stage, then serve warm on top of slice of pudding. Top off with large dollop of whipped cream, if desired.

Mom's Dessert Was a Labor of Love

I GREW UP in the 1930s and one of my family's favorite desserts was Mom's Elderberry Dumplings.

In the fall, she'd pick and can the berries. Then in the winter, she'd open a can of berries, put them in a pan with a little sugar and heat them up.

Once they were hot, she'd mix up the dumplings and put them on top of the berries. We had a wood stove and once in a while, juice would boil over the top of the pan and spit and sputter.

When the dumplings were done, we'd eat them with some sugar, milk, cinnamon or nutmeg. My mom must have spent hours picking, cleaning and canning those berries, but we never realized it at the time. I know now that a lot of love went into that delicious dessert.

—Barbara Hicks, Spartansburg, Pennsylvania

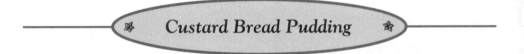

❀ Custard Bread Pudding ❀

Shared by Donna Johnson, Federal Way, Washington

3 eggs
1/4 cup sugar
1-1/2 slices white bread
2 cups milk
1 teaspoon vanilla
1/2 teaspoon salt
1/4 cup raisins
Cinnamon

Beat eggs. Blend in sugar, salt and vanilla. Add milk gradually while stirring mixture. Break bread into small pieces and mix into other ingredients. Stir in raisins. Pour into an 8- x 8-inch pan, distributing raisins evenly. Sprinkle cinnamon on top. Bake at 350° for about 30 to 35 minutes. This Custard Bread Pudding recipe can easily be doubled and put into an 8- x 12-inch pan. If doubling recipe, you will need to bake it a little longer.

Snow Ice Cream

Shared by Carole Talcott, Dahinda, Illinois

ICE CREAM *was a special treat during my childhood, but none was more special than snow ice cream. We made it to celebrate the first "good snow" of the year.*

After mixing up the ingredients, we'd head out into the snow with our bowl and add clean, fresh snow to the mixture until it thickened.

Even though my children and grandchildren have easy access to ice cream in their freezers, they still look forward to this traditional treat!

2 eggs, beaten
6 tablespoons sugar
1-1/2 cups half and half
1-1/2 teaspoons vanilla

In a large bowl, add sugar to eggs and beat well. Add half and half and vanilla. Cook over low heat, stirring constantly, until slightly thickened. Chill. Put on your boots and wade out in the snow with your bowl of the mixture and a large mixing spoon. Add enough clean, fresh snow to mixture to make it thick. Eat immediately. **Yield: 4** generous or 6 small servings.

Caramel Squares

Shared by Darcy McCarron, Chester, Nova Scotia

1-1/2 cups brown sugar, *divided*
1/2 cup margarine *or* butter
2 eggs, *separated*
1 teaspoon vanilla
1-1/2 cups flour
2 teaspoons baking powder

Mix all the above ingredients except the egg whites and 1 cup of the brown sugar. Press mixture into a 9- x 9-inch square pan. Beat the egg whites until stiff and add the remaining brown sugar. Beat well until sugar is dissolved. Spread over mixture in pan and bake at 325° for 20 minutes.

Depression Pudding

Shared by Grace Gaspar, Springtown, Pennsylvania

I SPENT MOST of the Depression years on a farm where milk was plentiful.

Our friends from town weren't so lucky, but they did receive bags of rice from the government. So we came up with the idea to trade! We gave them milk for some of their rice and the result was rice pudding—lots of it—on our table through those hard years.

These days, when I know my sister is stopping by, I include a special item on my menu—a big bowl of Depression Pudding. It always gives us a laugh.

8 tablespoons white rice
2 quarts milk
5 tablespoons sugar
1/2 teaspoon salt
1 cup seedless raisins, optional
1 teaspoon vanilla
Cinnamon

Rinse rice in cool water. Put in large baking dish with milk, sugar, salt and raisins, if desired. Sprinkle top with cinnamon. Bake in 325° oven for about 1-1/2 hours or until rice comes to top. Remove from oven several times to stir while baking. Add vanilla when rice is tender and pudding is finished.

Indian Pudding

Shared by Janice Harvey, Grafton, New Hampshire

2/3 cup yellow cornmeal
1 teaspoon ground ginger
1 teaspoon salt
4-1/2 cups milk
1 cup molasses
Ice cream *or* whipped cream

In top of double boiler, mix all ingredients except ice cream or whipped cream. Place over boiling water and steam for 2 hours. Serve warm. Top with vanilla ice cream or whipped cream. **Yield:** 8 servings.

Grandma's Graham Pudding

Shared by Ethel Quillin, Chula Vista, California

1 tablespoon shortening,
  melted, *or* olive oil
1 cup molasses
1 cup milk
1 cup raisins
2 cups graham flour
1-1/2 teaspoons baking soda
1 teaspoon cinnamon
1 teaspoon salt

Sauce
2 cups water
1/2 teaspoon salt
1 cup sugar
1-1/2 tablespoons cornstarch
1 teaspoon allspice
1/2 teaspoon cinnamon
1/4 teaspoon cloves

Bring all ingredients to a boil and cook until clear and thickened. Serve hot.

Mix dry ingredients and raisins. Combine shortening, molasses and milk. Add to dry mixture and stir until evenly moistened. Pour into greased, floured loaf pan to bake or into a greased container with tight-fitting lid (like a coffee can) to steam. If steaming, place a cloth over the top of the can before putting on the tight-fitting lid. This prevents steam from dripping off the inside of the lid onto the pudding and making it soggy. Steam or bake pudding in slow oven at 275° for 1-1/2 hours. Test with a toothpick to be certain center is done. Serve hot or cold with sugar and cream or prepare this spicy sauce using the following recipe.

Noodle Pudding

Shared by Reina Feder, West Haverstraw, New York

1 8-ounce package medium
   noodles
5 eggs
3/4 cup sugar
1/2 teaspoon salt
1 16-ounce container
   sour cream
3 large Cortland apples,
   sliced 1/4 inch thick, *or*
   1 can apple pie filling
2 teaspoons vanilla
1/2 cup raisins

3/4 stick butter, melted
2 teaspoons cinnamon

Parboil noodles about 6 to 8 minutes. Beat eggs and sugar well. Add salt, sour cream, butter and vanilla and beat again. Fold in apples, raisins and cinnamon. Pour into lightly greased square glass dish. Sprinkle with cinnamon and sugar. Bake at 350° about 1 hour until well set and nicely browned on all sides.

Vinegar Pie

Shared by Malinda Ledbetter, Carmi, Illinois

4 tablespoons flour
1 cup sugar, *divided*
2 cups water, boiling
2 eggs, *separated*
1 tablespoon butter
3 tablespoons vinegar
1 teaspoon lemon extract,
   optional

Mix flour with 1/2 cup sugar. Add water and cook for 15 minutes. Add the remaining 1/2 cup sugar and beaten egg yolks and cook a few minutes longer. Stir in butter, vinegar and lemon extract, if desired. Make a pie meringue with egg whites and spread over pie. Cover pie and brown in oven 12 to 15 minutes.

Oatmeal Drop Cookies

Shared by Agnes Cassity, Beaver, Oklahoma

1 cup sugar
1/2 cup butter
1/2 cup lard
1 cup raisins
1/2 cup water
1 teaspoon cinnamon
2 eggs, beaten
1 teaspoon baking soda
1 teaspoon vanilla
2 cups flour
2 cups oatmeal
1 cup nutmeats

Sift flour, then measure. Sift flour and cinnamon together. Cream sugar, butter and lard. Add beaten eggs. Cook raisins in 1/2 cup water. Drain and reserve water. Add baking soda to water and stir into creamed mixture. Stir in oatmeal, then flour and cinnamon. Add raisins, nutmeats and vanilla. Drop teaspoonfuls of dough onto greased cookie sheet and flatten with a fork dipped in cold water. Bake at 350° for about 15 minutes. **Yield:** 3 dozen.

Mom's Sugar Cookies Helped Bring in Money During Hard Times

WHEN I WAS *a little girl, my dad worked as a butcher. At the store where he worked, the dairy department was next to the meat counter.*

In those days they didn't sell sour cream—they dumped it. So when the milkman came to take away the old milk and cream, my dad would ask for the sour cream. My mom would use it to make big sugar cookies.

My sister and I would take a box with a white cloth and stacks of her delicious cookies and sell them for 10 cents a dozen. That's how my mother helped supplement our income during the Depression.

—Audrey Cleveland, Orland, California

❧ Grandmother's Buttermilk Pie ❧

Shared by Ruby Williams, Bogalusa, Louisiana

1 cup sugar
3 tablespoons flour
1/4 teaspoon salt
3 eggs, *separated*
2 cups buttermilk
4 tablespoons butter, melted
1 teaspoon lemon extract
1 unbaked pie shell

In a large bowl mix together sugar, flour and salt. Add egg yolks, buttermilk, butter and lemon extract. Fold in stiffly beaten egg whites. Pour into pie shell. Place in 450° oven for 5 minutes, then reduce heat to 350° and bake 45 minutes.

❧ Tomato Soup Cake ❧

Shared by Kathy Porter, Dilmar, Delaware

2 cups flour, sifted
1 teaspoon baking soda
2 teaspoons baking powder
1 teaspoon cinnamon
1 teaspoon nutmeg
1/2 teaspoon cloves
1/2 cup shortening
1 cup sugar
1 can tomato soup
1 cup walnuts, chopped, optional
1 cup raisins

Add dry ingredients and soup alternately. Stir in nuts and raisins. Mix all by hand. Put in greased and floured loaf pan. Bake for 50 to 60 minutes at 350°. Let stand 24 hours before cutting.

Optional Cream Cheese Icing
3 ounces cream cheese
1-1/2 cups confectioners' sugar, sifted
1 teaspoon vanilla

Sift dry ingredients 3 times. Cream shortening and sugar until fluffy.

Mix together. Spread on Tomato Soup Cake.

Strawberry Hash

Shared by Theresa Bibeau, Alturas, California

AS A MINISTER'S wife, Grandma often helped make food for church socials and potluck dinners.

During the 1930s, most of the women in the congregation had gardens and they grew strawberries every year. For summer events, they'd get together and make Strawberry Hash.

Cooking oil was hard to come by, so those resourceful ladies used layers of soda crackers to put together the "crust" for a tasty treat that gained quite a following in the area. They used a galvanized washtub to make enough of the dessert to feed the whole congregation.

When I was growing up, my family made Strawberry Hash every Fourth of July and now I make it every summer with my own children.

6 pints fresh strawberries
2 cups sugar
1 box soda crackers,
    unsalted, rinsed
Whipped cream, optional

Wash, hull and slice berries. Place in a large bowl. Pour sugar over berries and mash with potato masher. Mash the berries lightly, just enough to make them soft and juicy. In a large glass bowl, layer crackers and 1/2 to 1 cup berries. Repeat layers until bowl is full. Cover and chill in refrigerator overnight or for 24 hours. The crackers should soak up the juice and be like a thick pudding-pie or cake. When ready to serve, top with whipped cream, if desired.

Grandma's Rock Cookies

Shared by Myrtle Dawson, Elk River, Minnesota

1 cup sugar
1/2 cup butter *or* margarine
1/2 cup shortening
2 eggs
1/2 cup buttermilk
1 teaspoon baking soda
1 teaspoon salt
1/2 teaspoon cloves
1 teaspoon cinnamon
1 cup raisins, soaked in hot

water and drained
2 cups flour
2 cups oatmeal
1/2 cup nuts, optional

Mix raisins in flour and oatmeal. Then add ingredients in order given. Mix well. Drop by tablespoonfuls onto greased cookie sheet. Bake at 375° for 10 to 12 minutes.

Sour Cream Raisin Pie

Shared by Eileen Claeys, Long Grove, Iowa

1 9-inch unbaked pie shell
Raisins, enough to cover bottom
of pie shell
3 eggs, *separated*
1 cup sour cream
1 cup sugar
1 tablespoon cornstarch
Pinch salt
1 teaspoon cinnamon
1 teaspoon cloves

Meringue
2 egg whites

1/4 teaspoon salt
2 tablespoons sugar

Cover bottom of pie shell with raisins. Mix egg yolks, sour cream, sugar, cornstarch, salt, cinnamon and cloves. Pour over raisins in pie shell. Bake at 350° for 1 hour. To make meringue, combine ingredients. Beat until stiff. Spread over pie and brown in oven.

Depression Cake

Shared by Ruth Rutten, Bainbridge Island, Washington

MY FATHER was a Rawleigh salesman from 1927 to 1939. His product line included spices, vanilla, cosmetics, liniments and many other items. The kids were happy to see him pull up in his Model T Ford truck, since he always gave them gum and candy.

Money was scarce, so Dad bartered with the farmers on his route for eggs, chickens, beef and pork.

We kept a side of beef and some pork on the glassed-in front porch we used as our freezer through the frigid North Dakota winters. The vegetables Mom canned from our garden helped see us through the cold weather.

Mom canned beef cubes which she used to make stew. We'd always have mashed potatoes and hot baking powder biscuits with our stew. For dessert, Mom would serve one of my favorites—Depression Cake. That simple meal was one of the best Mom made...for us and for company.

2 cups brown sugar
2/3 cup shortening
2 cups water
4 cups raisins
2 teaspoons cinnamon
1 teaspoon cloves
1 teaspoon nutmeg
1/2 teaspoon allspice
1 teaspoon salt
2 teaspoons baking soda
4 cups flour
2 teaspoons baking powder
1-1/2 cups walnuts, optional

Combine first 9 ingredients in a saucepan. Bring to a boil and boil for 3 minutes, stirring constantly. Cool. Sift together baking soda, flour and baking powder. Add sifted ingredients to mixture while it's still lukewarm. Mix well. Add walnuts, if desired. Pour into 2 well-greased and floured loaf pans or a 9- x 13-inch cake pan. Bake at 350° for 45 minutes or longer. Check for doneness with a toothpick. No frosting necessary.

Butter and Cream Pie

Shared by Malinda Ledbetter, Carmi, Illinois

1 cup sugar
2 eggs
1/2 cup butter
1/4 cup cream
1 teaspoon vanilla *or* dash nutmeg
1 unbaked pie shell

Mix ingredients well. Line medium-size pan with pie shell. Pour in mixture and bake at 400° for 20 minutes. Then reduce temperature to 350° and bake for 3 minutes more.

Mock Pecan Pie

Shared by Elizabeth Willhite, Springfield, Missouri

2 eggs
3/4 cup sugar
3/4 cup dark syrup
3/4 cup oats
1/4 teaspoon salt
1/4 pound butter *or* oleo, melted
1 teaspoon vanilla
1 unbaked pie shell

Beat eggs well. Add remaining ingredients, folding in oats last. Pour in pie shell and bake at 350° for 30 to 35 minutes.

Grandma Ward's Molasses Cookies

Shared by Kristine Pryor, South Jordan, Utah

EVERY AUTUMN I make a batch of Grandma Ward's Molasses Cookies and relive a special memory.

I grew up on a potato farm in southeast Idaho and each fall when we'd dig the spuds, Grandma would bring us these cookies for break time.

We could count on having them at least once during the harvest. She frosted them with a thin layer of "water frosting" and she always made them extra big to satisfy her hungry workers.

I'm not a coffee drinker, but I make sure to have some on hand so I can take a stroll down memory lane with these special cookies.

1 cup shortening
2 cups sugar
1 egg
2 teaspoons vanilla
1 cup molasses
3 teaspoons ginger
3 teaspoons baking soda
1 cup hot coffee
Dash salt
7 to 8 cups all-purpose flour *or* half white and half wheat flour

Water Frosting
2 cups confectioners' sugar
1 teaspoon vanilla
1/8 teaspoon lemon extract, optional
7 to 8 tablespoons water

Cream shortening, sugar, egg and vanilla. Add molasses and ginger. Dissolve baking soda in coffee and add to mixture. It should be a very runny consistency. Add dash of salt and mix in flour 1 to 2 cups at a time until dough can be handled but is still slightly sticky. Roll out about 1/4 inch thick on lightly floured surface. Cut out cookies. Bake at 375° for about 7 minutes. Cool. To make Water Frosting, mix ingredients until smooth. Add water to make a glaze that won't run off the cookies. Spread on cooled cookies. **Yield:** about 7 dozen.

Hard Times Cake

Shared by Frances Elliott, Sundown, Texas

MOTHER baked her Hard Times Cake for me and my eight brothers and sisters often when we were growing up.

She baked it in a big iron skillet in her wood-burning stove and I still have memories of how good it tasted fresh from the oven.

We always had to wait for Dad to get home from work before we could dig into the cake. It was hard to do sometimes and one day my oldest brother decided to try and sneak a piece of cake.

My mother caught him and made him finish the whole thing himself. He never wanted that kind of cake again!

1/2 cup butter
2 cups sugar
1 cup sour cream
3 cups flour
3 eggs

1/2 teaspoon baking soda

Mix ingredients together. Bake cake in layers and spread with jelly when cool.

Mother Had the Magic Touch with Strudel

MY MOTHER made strudel for us often when we were growing up on a farm in South Dakota.

She would make the dough in the center of a small table covered with a clean tablecloth. She'd pull and stretch the dough until it was paper-thin and covered the table. Then she would sprinkle melted butter, raisins, apples and cinnamon on it, roll it up and bake it.

After I got married, I tried to make it, but I just ended up with dough and lots of holes! —Ethel Jass, Roseville, Minnesota

Skillet Cake

Shared by Sherrie Wolf, Granger, Indiana

3   cups flour
2   cups sugar
2   tablespoons cocoa
1   teaspoon salt
2   teaspoons baking soda
2   tablespoons vanilla
2   tablespoons vinegar
1/4 pound butter, melted
2   cups cold water

Preheat oven to 375°. Grease a 12-inch iron skillet. Sift flour, sugar, cocoa, salt and baking soda into it. After stirring dry ingredients together, take a wooden spoon and make 3 holes in them. Pour vanilla into one hole, vinegar into second hole and melted butter into last hole. Pour cold water over all and stir. Bake for 25 minutes.

Icing

1/8 pound butter
2/3 cup brown sugar
1/2 to 2/3 cup walnuts,
      ground
3   tablespoons canned milk
      or 2 tablespoons regular
      milk

Melt the butter in a saucepan and stir in brown sugar. Add walnuts and canned or regular milk. Stir well. Pour over cake as soon as cake is done and put under broiler about 5 minutes or until it bubbles.

Mom's Crispy Turnovers Were Simply Delicious

MY MOM DIDN'T make many cakes or pies, but she did make fruit cobblers which are still my favorite today.

She also had one special recipe she'd make when she was running low on ingredients. She would make biscuit dough, roll it out, lay a saucer on top of it and cut out circles.

Next, she'd put a layer of butter, sugar and cinnamon on the pieces, fold them in half and bake them until they were brown and crusty. She would make a milk sauce and pour it over those brown turnovers before she served them.

The dough stayed crispy, but the milk seeped down inside and they tasted like heaven! I've tried to make those turnovers too, but I can't seem to duplicate them. —Helen O'Key, Litchfield, Connecticut

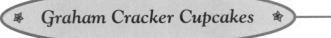

Graham Cracker Cupcakes

Shared by Betty Barnhill, Baudette, Minnesota

1/2 cup shortening
1 cup sugar
2 eggs, *separated,* beaten
3/4 cup milk
3 cups graham cracker crumbs
1-1/2 teaspoons baking powder
3 tablespoons flour
1 cup nuts
Dash salt
1 teaspoon vanilla

Cream shortening and sugar. Add egg yolks. Stir and add milk. Mix together cracker crumbs, baking powder, flour, nuts and dash of salt. Combine dry ingredients with liquid and mix in vanilla. Add egg whites and mix well. Pour mixture into cupcake liners in muffin pans. Bake at 350° for 25 minutes. **Yield:** 2 dozen cupcakes. These cupcakes are very good with cream cheese frosting.

Cottage Cheese Pie

Shared by Judy Matti, Stevensville, Montana

1 12-ounce carton creamed
   cottage cheese
1/4 teaspoon salt
3/4 cup sugar
2 eggs, lightly beaten
Milk to fill pie tin
1 9-inch pastry for double
   crust pie
Dash nutmeg

Blend all ingredients together. Pour mixture into pie shell. Then sprinkle the top of the pie with nutmeg. Bake at 350° as you would a custard pie until a knife blade inserted in center comes out clean. Cool pie and refrigerate until served.

Breakfast Cookies

Shared by Sandra Britt, Sonoma, California

GRANDMA *made her special cookies for Grandpa on Saturdays and he ate one or two every morning for breakfast. Originally she baked them with lard.*

These days I make Grandma's cookies for my grandchildren and have been known to serve them at breakfast now and then.

1 cup margarine *or*
   shortening
1 cup sugar, white *or* brown
   or half and half
1 cup molasses
1 egg
1 tablespoon cinnamon
1 tablespoon ground ginger
5 cups flour
1 teaspoon salt
1 teaspoon baking soda
1 cup water
1 to 2 cups raisins

Cream margarine and sugar. Beat in molasses and egg. Mix cinnamon, ginger, flour, salt and baking soda. Add dry ingredients alternately with water to creamed mixture. Mix in raisins. Drop by spoonfuls onto ungreased cookie sheet. Bake at 350° for 10 to 15 minutes.

Blueberry Boy Bait

Shared by Phyllis Buchner, LaPorte, Indiana

WHEN I was younger, my grandmother gave me her secret recipe for Blueberry Boy Bait and over the years it worked for me and my daughters!

My girls worked in the blueberry fields, so we had plenty of fresh and frozen berries year round. I baked on Saturdays, and there would always be a knock at the door shortly after I put a pan of these bars in the oven.

Often the young fellows would have a question about homework or used some other excuse for dropping by. But it was obvious they knew that something good would be coming out of the oven soon!

2 cups flour
1-1/2 cups sugar
3/4 cup shortening
2 eggs, *separated*
1 cup milk
1 teaspoon vanilla
1 pint fresh blueberries *or*

1 can blueberries, drained

Blend flour, sugar and shortening with pastry cutter until it resembles coarse meal. Remove 1 cup for topping and set aside. Add egg yolks, milk and vanilla to creamed mixture and blend until smooth. Beat egg whites until stiff, then gently fold into mixture. Pour into greased 9- x 13-inch pan. Place blueberries evenly on top of batter and top with reserved crumb mixture. Bake at 350° for 40 minutes.

THE
RIGHT
FLOUR

Surrounding the gluten and starch cells in the wheat berry there is a layer of almost pure white fibre.   It is called cellulose and is as indigestible as sawdust. The presence of cellulose in flour cannot be detected except by special test.   But it makes a difference in the moisture absorbing quality and so lessens the number of loaves to the sack.   Some millers permit cellulose to go into their flour, but it is eliminated from GOLD MEDAL FLOUR by our special purifying process.

Washburn-Crosby's
GOLD MEDAL FLOUR

Charlene Wheeler

Rainy Days Were Spent in the Kitchen with Mom

DURING THE DEPRESSION, my family headed out west from our home in Minnesota and found work following the crops and picking. Some jobs were backbreaking and some were fun—at least as a child I thought they were.

Some of my fondest memories are of the rainy days I spent with my mom. We'd get out the recipe box in the morning and decide what to bake.

We'd discard some recipes because we had no eggs or were running low on sugar. Some required other jobs to be done first, like rendering lard for pie crust, and were quickly eliminated.

Once we even rejected a recipe because Mom was mad at the woman who gave it to her. I was glad when they made up though, because that sure was a good cake!

My grandmother was famous for her flaky pie crusts. Her secret was lard. She didn't use a recipe though, so I don't know the amounts she added. Now I find myself doing the same thing—just dumping ingredients in the bowl. —B.J. DeWitt, Lakeview, Oregon

---

❧ Grandma's Frosted Creams ❧

Shared by June Formanek, Belle Plaine, Iowa

1/2 cup sugar
1 cup shortening
2 eggs, beaten
1 cup sorghum
1/2 cup sour milk
2 teaspoons baking soda
3 tablespoons vinegar
3 cups flour

1 teaspoon cloves
1 teaspoon allspice
1 teaspoon cinnamon
1/2 cup raisins, optional
1/2 cup nuts, optional

Cream together sugar and shortening. Blend in beaten eggs. Add

180

sorghum and sour milk and mix well. Dissolve baking soda in the vinegar and add to the first mixture. Combine flour and spices and blend into the batter. If desired, add 1/2 cup each raisins and/or nuts. Pour into a 10- x 15-inch cookie sheet that has been lightly greased. Bake at 350° for 35 to 40 minutes. When cool, top with frosting or glaze, if desired. These are especially good served with vanilla ice cream.

✽❀✿✽❀✿✽❀✿✽

Burnt Sugar Cake

Shared by Marjorie Moore, Watsonville, California

  1/2 cup shortening
1-1/2 cups sugar
    2 eggs, *separated*
    1 cup water
2-1/2 cups flour, *divided*
    2 teaspoons baking powder
Pinch salt
    1 teaspoon vanilla

Burnt Sugar
  1/2 cup sugar
    1 cup water

Frosting
    6 tablespoons brown sugar
    5 tablespoons milk *or* cream
Vanilla
Confectioners' sugar

Cream shortening and sugar. Add well-beaten egg yolks, water and 2 cups of flour. Beat until smooth. For burnt sugar, heat sugar in heavy saucepan until black. Add water and boil to a syrup. Reserve 1 tablespoon of syrup for frosting. Add remaining syrup to creamed mixture with remaining flour, baking powder and salt. Beat well and add vanilla. Beat egg whites until stiff and fold into cake mixture. Pour into 2 greased and floured cake pans. Bake at 325° for 25 to 30 minutes or until cake tests done. For frosting, bring brown sugar and milk to boil. Remove from heat and add reserved burnt sugar and vanilla to taste. Thicken with confectioners' sugar. Frost cake and enjoy.

181

Chocolate Jumbles

Shared by Mrs. Harry Zea, Avon, New York

ONE OF THE happiest memories of my childhood is of watching my mother making her delicious Chocolate Jumbles. They were a staple in our house—an after-school snack with a glass of milk or a treat to take to an ailing neighbor.

Mother always mixed the dough the night before baking day so it could stiffen without extra flour. She'd roll out the dough and cut it with a doughnut cutter, making a hole in the center of each cookie.

As she gathered up the centers for re-rolling, she always let me snitch a few to eat. After the cookies were done, she'd ice them with frosting made of confectioners' sugar and water.

My grandchildren still ask for these cookies today and I always include them in the care packages I send. As I sit in my kitchen and frost those cookies, I recall many happy days with my mother.

    1 cup cocoa
    2 cups molasses
    1 cup brown sugar
    1 cup shortening
    2 eggs
  1/2 cup hot water
1-1/2 teaspoons baking soda
    1 teaspoon cinnamon
    1 teaspoon cloves
Dash salt
4-1/2 to 5 cups flour

Stir baking soda into water. Then mix ingredients together. Roll dough to 1/2-inch thickness on floured board and cut with doughnut cutter. Bake approximately 10 to 12 minutes at 350°. Frost on bottom with icing made of confectioners' sugar and water.

❊ *Royal Rhubarb Custard Pie* ❊

Shared by Darlene Tenaglia, Bellingham, Washington

2 cups rhubarb, finely
  chopped
1-1/4 cups sugar
2 tablespoons flour
1 tablespoon cornstarch
2 tablespoons melted butter
2 egg yolks, beaten
1 teaspoon vanilla
1 9-inch unbaked pie shell

Meringue
2 egg whites
1/4 cup sugar

1/2 teaspoon vanilla
Cream of tartar

Mix first 7 ingredients in order given. Let stand 30 minutes. (Mixture will look thickened.) Pour into pie shell and bake at 375° for 45 minutes. Remove from oven. For meringue, combine ingredients and beat until stiff. Cover pie with meringue and bake at 400° for 10 minutes. Remove from oven and cool. **Yield:** 6 servings.

Fresh Dairy Products Were Secret to Mom's Baking

I'LL NEVER be able to duplicate the rich desserts my mother made when I was growing up—not without her secret ingredients.

On baking day, she'd go to the milk house and skim off pure cream from our Holstein cows. She also used homemade butter in all her baking.

After being away from farm cooking for 40 years, I recently tasted homemade butter again. The fresh milk was churned into butter which we spread on slices of homemade bread straight from the oven.

I realize now that we ate like royalty growing up on that farm!
—Gail Ritsema-Cowles, Milton, Wisconsin

Nannie's Gingerbread

Shared by Saxon White, Boise, Idaho

NANNIE *traveled from Nebraska to Idaho in a covered wagon in 1900 with Grandpa, her parents and several of her 13 siblings.*

She brought her gingerbread recipe with her and baked it in her wood-burning stove all her life. It was a filling treat during the Depression.

Nannie had very few written recipes since she did most of her cooking from memory. So her gingerbread is a special treat for our family.

1/2 cup butter *or* margarine
1/2 cup sugar
1 egg, beaten
1 cup molasses
2-1/2 cups flour
1-1/2 teaspoons baking soda
1 teaspoon cinnamon
1/2 teaspoon cloves
1 teaspoon ginger
1/2 teaspoon salt
1 cup hot water
Whipped cream

Cream butter and sugar. Add egg and molasses. Sift dry ingredients and blend into creamed mixture. Add hot water and beat until smooth. Bake in shallow 8- x 10-inch pan at 350° for about 35 minutes. When cool, top with whipped cream.

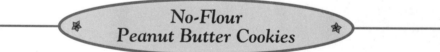

No-Flour Peanut Butter Cookies

Shared by Cynthia Sudsbury, Milbridge, Maine

1 cup peanut butter
1 cup sugar
1 egg, lightly beaten
1 teaspoon baking soda
1 teaspoon vanilla

Mix all ingredients together. Mixture will be thick. Drop by teaspoonfuls onto greased cookie sheet. Flatten with a fork. Bake at 300° for 12 to 15 minutes. Let cookies stand briefly before removing to cooling rack. **Yield:** about 2 dozen.

Chapter 8.

Canned Foods

Vegetables, fruits and jams gave families much-needed "insurance" for the cold winters ahead.

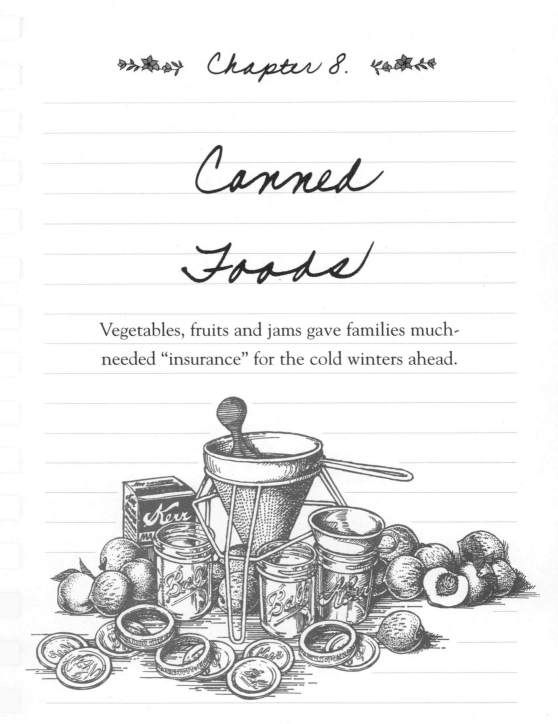

Mom's Ketchup

Shared by Grace Gaspar, Springtown, Pennsylvania

ONE of my favorite take-to-school lunches was a ketchup sandwich.

My mother would fill a small jelly jar with her homemade ketchup, wrap three or four slices of bread in waxed paper and put it all in my lunch sack with a spoon.

At lunchtime, I'd heap generous spoonfuls of ketchup on each bread slice, spread it around and sink my teeth into it. It was so good!

Sometimes I'd trade one of my ketchup sandwiches for one made with store-bought lunchmeat. Only the rich kids had lunchmeat sandwiches during the Depression, so they were rare. But those kids always enjoyed my Mom's homemade ketchup as much as I did!

    1 cup white vinegar
1-1/2 teaspoons whole cloves
1-1/2 teaspoons broken
      cinnamon stick
    1 teaspoon celery seed
    8 pounds tomatoes, crushed
    2 cups water
    1 tablespoon onion,
      chopped
  1/2 teaspoon cayenne pepper
    1 cup sugar
    4 teaspoons salt

In a saucepan combine vinegar, cloves, cinnamon and celery seed. Bring to a boil. Let stand 1 hour so vinegar can absorb spices. In a large kettle, mix tomatoes, water, onion and cayenne pepper. Boil for 15 minutes. Put through a sieve. Add sugar to hot tomato juice. Bring to a boil, stirring constantly until mixture reduces by half. Put vinegar mixture through a sieve to remove spices. Add vinegar and salt to tomato juice. Boil another 30 minutes, stirring the mixture constantly. Pour into hot jars or bottles. Consult a canning guide for processing directions.

Green Tomato Relish

Shared by A. Lee Hickman, Killen, Alabama

1 peck green tomatoes, chopped
1 cup salt
6 green peppers, chopped
5 sweet red peppers, chopped
6 medium onions, chopped
3 quarts vinegar
8 cups sugar
2 tablespoons celery seed
2 tablespoons mustard seed
1 tablespoon whole cloves

Place chopped green tomatoes in a colander and sprinkle with salt. Drain overnight. Discard liquid the next day. Combine remaining ingredients and add to tomatoes. Cook 20 minutes. Pack into hot sterile jars. Consult a canning guide for processing directions. These amounts may be reduced and ingredients cooked to serve as a side dish with meats and vegetables instead of canning.

Poke Stalk Pickles

Shared by Precious Owens, Elizabethtown, Kentucky

Poke stalks
　　1 pint vinegar
　　1/2 teaspoon mustard seed
　　2 tablespoons sugar
Water
Salt

Use only tender poke stalks less than 6 inches high. Cut stalks into 3-inch pieces. Trim off leaves. Cook in water about 5 minutes. Discard water. Cover again with salted water and boil about 5 minutes. Discard water. Pack stalks vertically in jars. Combine vinegar, mustard seed and sugar. Heat to boiling. Pour over pickles. Consult a canning guide for processing directions.

Corn Cob Jelly

Shared by Merrybell Seeber, Delavan, Wisconsin

12 corn cobs, bright red, dry, clean
3 pints water
1 package powdered pectin
3 cups sugar

Break up corn cobs and add to boiling water. Boil for 30 minutes. Remove from heat and strain through a cloth. Add enough water to make 3 cups of juice. Add powdered pectin and bring to a rolling boil. Stir in sugar and boil for 2 to 3 minutes or until it reaches jelly stage. Pour into jelly glasses. Consult a canning guide for processing directions.

Apple Butter

Shared by Betty Barrett, Grand Island, New York

12 pounds (about 4 dozen) apples, unpeeled
3 quarts sweet cider
6 cups brown sugar *or*
4 cups honey
Juice of 1 lemon
3 teaspoons ground cinnamon
1 teaspoon ground cloves
1/2 teaspoon ground allspice

Cook apples in cider until tender. Press through a food mill or sieve. Add brown sugar or honey, lemon juice and spices. Place in large enamel roasting pan in 300° oven. Cook slowly for several hours or perhaps overnight, stirring occasionally. Butter will thicken as it bakes. When it has thickened sufficiently, remove from oven and pack into hot sterilized jars, leaving 1/2 inch head space. Adjust lids. Consult a canning guide for processing directions. **Yield:** 10 to 12 pints.

Mother's Canned Food Was Good As 'Money in the Bank'

MOTHER'S cellar shelves were the "bank account" that got us through the Great Depression.

While waiting out the frequent Oklahoma thunderstorms—and the huge dust clouds that blew through ahead of them—I spent many hours in the cellar admiring the rows of colorful jars of food Mother and I had canned during summer.

Those jars contained all different kinds of vegetables as well as peaches and pears gathered from the trees in our community. Pickles, relishes, sauerkraut, jams and jellies stood in rows.

My job was to help pick, snap, shell, peel or skin the fruits and vegetables. Often I ran to the country store a block away to buy sugar, turmeric, vinegar, lids or jar rings. I also did my fair share of scrubbing and sterilizing fruit jars in vats of water which were drawn from the well.

Mother kept the fire going in the wood-burning range, sliced and diced, watched the gauge on the pressure cooker and ladled bubbling hot food into dozens of jars. We did all of this during the midday summer heat since we had no electricity for lights.

The next day, after we'd turned each jar upside down to check for a safe seal, we'd place them in the big gray dishpan. Then I'd carefully carry them down to the cellar and arrange them on the shelves my father built.

The jars on those shelves helped feed us through the year, but they also represented more. For several years, my mother made meals for four of the local schoolteachers, using her earnings for our grocery money. Much of the food she served the teachers was what we'd canned ourselves.

More than once, a jar of pickles became my admission to the traveling picture show that rolled into our little town each fall.

It was on those days—and each time we sat down to eat—we were especially thankful for our "bank account" on those cellar shelves.
—Maurine Carter, Ventura, California

14-Day Sweet Pickles

Shared by Alice Pixler, Whiting, Iowa

3-1/2 quarts (about 4 pounds)
cucumbers, 2 inches long
1 cup coarse pickling salt
2 quarts water
1/2 teaspoon alum
5 cups vinegar
4-1/2 cups sugar, *divided*
2 tablespoons mixed
pickling spice

Wash cucumbers and cut in half lengthwise. Place in a large stone crock or jar. Dissolve salt in boiling water and pour over cucumbers. Cover and let stand a week.

8th day: drain and cover cucumbers with fresh boiling water.

9th day: drain and pour 2 quarts boiling water with alum over cucumbers.

10th day: drain and cover with fresh boiling water.

11th day: drain. Mix vinegar, pickling spice and 3 cups sugar. Heat to boiling. Pour over cucumbers.

12th day: drain and save liquid. Reheat liquid, add 1/2 cup sugar and pour over cucumbers.

13th day: repeat 12th day.

14th day: drain and add 1/2 cup sugar. Pack pickles in jars and pour boiling liquid over them. Consult a canning guide for processing directions.

Preserved Sauerkraut Made Tasty Winter Meals

ONE OF MY *most vivid memories of the 1930s is of my parents making sauerkraut in the fall. My father always used his homemade cabbage grater and wooden mallet.*

My parents shredded the cabbage, layered it with salt and beat it with the mallet until a barrel was full. We kept the barrel in the garage where it froze solid during winter.

On the weekends, my mother would chop a hunk of cabbage out of the barrel and cook it with a piece of pork butt. We would eat those delicious meals for 2 or 3 days. —Stephanie Heise, Rochester, New York

Green Tomato Mincemeat

Shared by Betty Albrecht, Newton, Illinois

1 gallon green tomatoes, chopped
1 gallon apples, cored and chopped
4 pints sugar
2 cups vinegar
1/2 cup flour
3 boxes raisins
1/2 cup butter

1/2 tablespoon pepper
1 tablespoon salt
4 tablespoons cinnamon

Mix all ingredients together and boil for 30 minutes. Pack into hot canning jars. Consult a canning guide for processing directions. **Yield:** 4 quarts.

Mom Put Her Canning Skills to Work

MY MOTHER *was very creative when it came to making sure her seven children were fed during the hard Depression years.*

We grew most of our food and Mom canned everything she could. About 1936, she learned how to use a pressure canner and was hired to be part of a government-sponsored relief program that provided canned food for people in our county.

The pressure canner, lid sealer, cans and lids were furnished as part of the program. Mom would go to other people's houses and can their fruits and vegetables in exchange for a portion of the food for the county to give to needy families. It was a very innovative program at the time.

Mom received a salary from the county for her work, but I'm not sure how much it was. I do know that the extra money helped us get through those tough times—and helped other families in the process.

—Dorothy Adcock, Smithville, Tennessee

Shared by Delaine Stolpa, La Crosse, Wisconsin

Beans
Beets
Carrots
Peaches *or* watermelon rind
    1 cup white vinegar
    1 cup sugar
  1/2 cup water

Spice bag
    1 teaspoon cinnamon

1/2 teaspoon allspice
1/2 teaspoon cloves

Cook vegetables until tender. For 1 quart, mix vinegar, sugar and water and boil with spice bag for 10 minutes. Add drained vegetables and heat to boiling. Pack into sterilized jars. Consult a canning guide for processing directions.

Making Jelly Called for Creative Measures

MAKING JELLY *during the Depression was difficult for many people because sugar was expensive.*

We were fortunate to have an orchard and wild blackberries, plums, elderberries and gooseberries, but we had to save money for sugar and bought only small amounts at a time.

Before pectin was available, you had to boil the fruit juice until it was nearly half gone before it jelled. It was a long, hot job, but worth the effort! —Pauline Longnecker, West Plains, Missouri

Shared by Nina Egeland, Colts Neck, New Jersey

I WAS BORN in a town along the Navesink River near Sandy Hook, New Jersey, and my family enjoyed many meals from the clams, fish and oysters we caught there.

My Pop would rake the hard clams from his oyster boat named "The Nina". He'd wash them off and shuck them—saving the juice, of course.

Then he'd give all those fresh clams to Mom so she could make clam pie from Granny's recipe. These days, I have to be satisfied making the dish from canned clams, but my family loves it just the same.

We never served a side vegetable with clam pie since nothing seemed to go well with it. Instead, we all enjoyed a favorite taste treat—Sharon's Pickled Green Beans. You can take the jar off the shelf and it doesn't require any additional time when preparing your meal.

---

2 **pounds tender green beans**
1/2 **teaspoon cayenne pepper**
1-1/2 **tablespoons dill seed**
2-1/2 **cups water**
1 **garlic clove, split**
1/4 **cup salt**
2-1/2 **cups vinegar**

Stem the green beans (fresh from garden or market). Fill 4 pint jars with beans standing lengthwise. Leave 1/4 inch space at top. Bring the water, vinegar, pepper, dill, garlic and salt to boil. Pour over beans, leaving small air space. Consult a canning guide for processing directions.

Ripe Tomato Chutney

Shared by Barb Anderson, Deer Park, Wisconsin

1 cup green peppers,
  chopped
4 cups ripe tomatoes,
  chopped
2 cups green tomatoes,
  chopped
4 cups apples, chopped
1/2 cup onion, chopped
2 tablespoons mustard seed
2 tablespoons celery seed
1 teaspoon ground ginger

3 tablespoons salt
2 cups sugar
1 teaspoon cinnamon
1 teaspoon cloves
4 cups vinegar

Mix all of the ingredients and boil gently for 1-1/4 hours. Pack the mixture into hot canning jars. Consult a canning guide for processing directions.

Indian Sauce

Shared by Mary Stanley, Tulsa, Oklahoma

6 large ripe tomatoes,
  chopped
6 medium apples, chopped
2 quarts vinegar
1/2 pound seeded raisins
1/4 cup salt
2-1/2 cups brown sugar
1 medium pepper, chopped
3 medium onions, chopped
2 tablespoons ground
  mustard
1 tablespoon ginger

Mix all ingredients except the spices. Boil slowly for 1 hour. Run through a sieve. Add the spices and boil until thick. Stir as needed to prevent burning. Pour into hot sterilized jars. Consult a canning guide for processing directions.

Beet Pickles

Shared by Barbara Boser, Unity, Saskatchewan

Beets
- 5 cups sugar
- 5 cups white vinegar
- 1 tablespoon pickling salt
- 1/4 teaspoon cloves

Spray of dill

Boil all ingredients except beets. Pour mixture over beets. Adding dill gives the beets a good flavor.

Mother Burned the Midnight Oil To Keep the Pantry Stocked

DURING THE DEPRESSION, my mother and father grew and raised most of the food for our family.

We always had plenty to eat because Dad was a good gardener who could raise anything. He grew vegetables, raspberries, strawberries and peaches.

Besides the more common vegetables like radishes, beans, tomatoes and cabbage, Dad grew some more unusual items including oyster plants and celery. Of course, Mother's job was to preserve the extras for winter eating.

Many nights I can remember her staying up late to take the quarts of green beans out of the boiler and set them on the counter to cool before putting them with the others in our big storage closet.

Vegetables that Mother didn't can were stored outdoors between layers of dirt and straw. They kept well and it was always fun to bring in a fresh head of cabbage, carrots, squash or onions during the cold winter months. —Billie Hansberger, Cuba, Illinois

Elderberry Jelly

Shared by Mary Lund, South Stoddard, New Hampshire

5 **quarts ripe elderberries**
Juice of 2 lemons
5 **pounds sugar**

Place berries in a saucepan and crush. Heat gently and simmer for 15 minutes. Squeeze out the juice in a jelly bag. Put the juice (about 3 cups) in a pan with the lemon juice. Add sugar and mix well. Bring to a boil and boil gently for 20 minutes. Test on a plate. If spoonful does not thicken in a few seconds, boil another 5 minutes. Pour into jelly glasses. Consult a canning guide for processing directions.

Apple Chutney

Shared by Mona Turner, Midland, Texas

1 **teaspoon salt**
1/2 **pound raisins**
1/2 **pound onions, chopped**
3 **pints apples, chopped**
1 **cup brown sugar**
2 **cups water**
1 **cup cider vinegar**

Cardamom, cinnamon, ginger
and nutmeg to taste

Mix ingredients together, adding spices to taste. Cook well. Pour into hot sterilized jars. Consult a canning guide for processing directions.

Strawberry Patch Was Family Project

I REMEMBER how our family worked together to have a carpet of luscious red strawberries next to our vegetable garden.

We looked forward to the spring when we'd see the first blossoms on the plants. When the berries began to appear, Dad would carry milk cans full of water to the strawberry patch so we'd be assured a bountiful harvest.

Come June, my two sisters and I were eager to get out early in the morning to pick the berries—and of course, pop some of the biggest ones in our mouths. We would carry little wooden berry boxes to the kitchen where Mother would clean them with our little brother's help.

Mother got out her largest kettle and cooked the preserves on her old black range. She'd been saving jars for months and once the preserves were cooked to the proper thickness, into the jars they went. Then she sealed them up with paraffin—we kids always snitched some to chew on.

When winter came and we had hot soda biscuits to eat, we would top them with Mother's delicious strawberry preserves.

Grandmother also made preserves, but she had a different method. She would mix up huge pans of strawberries and sugar, cover them with fine mosquito netting and let them cook slowly under the hot sun for several days. She called them Sunshine Strawberry Preserves.

She had a matched set of glasses to put hers in and little tin lids to put on top, so we never got any paraffin scraps at her house. We did get to taste the preserves left in the pans though and Grandma's were also delicious!

—June Speer Chatteron,
Milan, Illinois

❦ Watermelon Rind Pickles ❦

Shared by Beulah Patterson, Marietta, Ohio

WHEN I WAS a little girl, my Grandma Hill taught me some important lessons—including how to get the most out of food.

One of my favorite childhood memories is eating Grandma's Watermelon Rind Pickles every summer.

Grandma raised five children of her own and then cared for me and my six siblings after our mother passed away. She was 65 years old when she took us in and the only income she had was from the farm that Grandpa had left her.

Money was tight, but Grandma was a go-getter. We raised a huge garden, had three milk cows and always had chickens and pigs. Grandma sold cream, butter and eggs so she could buy groceries and we never went to bed hungry.

Every year when we kids went to the Washington County Fair, Grandma would fix us a picnic lunch of fried chicken and those sweet and spicy pickles.

4-1/2 pounds (about 4 quarts) watermelon rind
6 tablespoons salt
3 quarts cold water, *divided*
2 tablespoons alum
1 quart white vinegar
9 cups sugar
1/4 cup whole cloves
2 cinnamon sticks, 3-inch pieces

To prepare watermelon rind, peel and remove all green and pink flesh. Cut into 1-inch cubes. Dissolve salt in 2 quarts of water. Pour over rind. Let stand 24 hours. Drain thoroughly. Dissolve alum in remaining water. Pour over rind. Let stand 24 hours. Drain thoroughly. Cover with fresh water. Let stand 24 hours. Bring rind to a boil in this water. Cook for 45 minutes until tender. Drain. Combine sugar and vinegar. Tie spices in cheesecloth bag. Add to sugar and vinegar mixture. Simmer about 10 minutes. Add watermelon rind. Cook for 30 to 40 minutes until clear and tender. Remove spice bag. Pack boiling hot into hot sterilized jars. Consult a canning guide for processing directions. **Yield:** 5 to 6 pints.

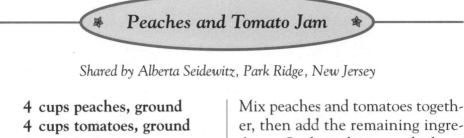

Peaches and Tomato Jam

Shared by Alberta Seidewitz, Park Ridge, New Jersey

4 cups peaches, ground
4 cups tomatoes, ground
8 cups sugar
1/2 cup lemon juice
1 stick cinnamon

Mix peaches and tomatoes together, then add the remaining ingredients. Cook until mixture thickens. Pour into hot jars. Consult a canning guide for processing directions. Can also be served on pancakes or waffles.

Mustard Pickles

Shared by Mae Wagner, Pickerington, Ohio

1 gallon cider vinegar
1 teaspoon saccharin
1/4 teaspoon alum
1 cup pure canning salt (no iodine)
1 cup granulated sugar
1 cup dry mustard
1/2 cup pickling spice
10 pounds whole pickles (not over 4 inches long)

Combine all ingredients but pickles. Bring mixture to a boil for 3 minutes. Pack pickles into sterilized hot quart jars. Pour boiling liquid over the pickles. Consult a canning guide for processing directions. Pickles will be ready to eat in 2-1/2 weeks.

Mom's Fruit Butters Were a Family Affair

I CAN STILL close my eyes and see my family in our 1930s kitchen, preparing apples, pears, peaches and plums for Mother's fruit butters.

If Dad wasn't busy in the fields or on a carpentry job, he'd be right in there peeling with the rest of us. He kept our minds busy with brain-teasers he made up. Sometimes, we'd sing to pass the time.

Mother would get out the huge copper kettle, shiny from a hot vinegar cleaning. Dad would start an outdoor fire and level the kettle on some bricks or stones. Then the all-day job would begin. We'd stir constantly and add sugar and spices while the fruit thickened.

When the fruit was done, we'd bring the kettle back into the kitchen and place it on blocks of wood on the table. Then Mother would dip the fruit butter into big stone jars that she'd cleaned and sterilized.

Since there was no paraffin to seal the jars, she'd place a sterile white cloth, cut to fit, directly on top of the butter and cover that with clean heavy paper, pasting it around the jar top.

Finally she'd cover it with several layers of white cloth and secure it with a strong cord. The butters kept well stored in a cool, dry place—and we enjoyed them all winter long!

—Sarah Holbert, Maidsville, West Virginia

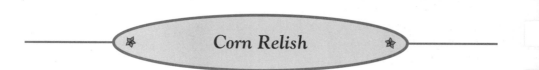

Corn Relish

Shared by Barb Anderson, Deer Park, Wisconsin

Corn, cut from 1 dozen ears
  1 head cabbage, chopped
  2 peppers, chopped
  1 cup sugar
  1/4 cup mustard

2 tablespoons salt

Stir the ingredients well. Cook for 30 minutes. Pack into hot canning jars. Consult a canning guide for processing directions.

Rose Hip Jelly

Shared by Mary Lund, South Stoddard, New Hampshire

Bagful of rose hips
Sugar
Water

Wash and dry the rose hips. Cut them in half lengthwise. Put them in a preserving kettle with a small amount of water. Cover and cook until tender, watching them to make sure they do not burn. Add a little more water if necessary. Strain through a jelly bag. Measure the liquid and add 1 pound of sugar for each pint of juice. Boil until mixture jells when a spoonful is tested on a plate. Pour into jelly glasses. Consult a canning guide for processing directions.

Unlabeled Cans Made for Mystery Meals

IN THE EARLY '30s, my parents, brother and I lived in the tiny Colorado town of Chivington.

One night, there was a big train crash—21 freight cars had broken through the trestle and piled up in the creek below. The cars were loaded with canned goods which were later given to people in the area.

The cans were dented and the creek water had soaked most of the labels off. The extra food helped us out, but it was a challenge for our mother. Whenever she opened a can, its contents were a surprise—it could be corn, tomatoes, peaches, fruit cocktail or any of a dozen other things. It sure made for some interesting meals!
—Louise Hines Dreher, Sun Lakes, Arizona

Long Days of Canning Were
Rewarded When the Snow Flew

ONE OF my earliest memories is of my mother and aunt canning corn at my grandmother's farm.

They always started around mid-July. Once the corn was ready, they chose the day and Dad would sharpen the knives the night before. We all got up at daybreak, and as a sleepy little girl, I knew we were in for a long day.

Everyone played a role in this family tradition. Dad and my uncle would go to the cornfield with bushel baskets while Mom and my aunt arranged the aluminum dishpans and knives in the summer kitchen. Grandmother was busy in the kitchen washing and scalding the jars.

Soon the first bushel arrived from the field. It would always be husked, but never clean enough to suit my mother. With a small brush and a cloth she made sure every bit of corn silk was gone.

Then they'd begin scraping the corn from the cobs. They could fill a dishpan faster than I could run to the barn to see my favorite calf! Mother would salt the corn and stir it with her hands until the corn was covered with foam. Then it went into Mason jars to be boiled in the big cooker.

A hundred pints later, we were always exhausted, but when the snow flew you couldn't find a better can of corn. Mother always served it in her yellow ware dish. Now that dish is displayed on my daughter's shelf.   —Bernadette Hugus Crooks, Clarion, Pennsylvania

Cherished Family Favorites

On these pages, you can preserve your
family's favorite old-fashioned recipes
handed down through the generations.

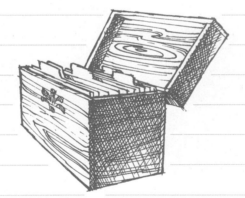